Ilivrid

WANDA PRICE

Print ISBN: 978-1-66781-4-278
eBook ISBN: 978-1-66781-4-285

Credit to my husband Henry L Price documentary commentator,
video production LightSource Production with Pastor Stan McCauley,
makeup artist front cover Adamo & Company Michael Adamo
and makeup artist back cover Tasheba Lawson.

Dedication

This dedication is to my Husband Henry L. Price who supported me to the end, all six of my children Daryl, Andrew, Alexis, Joshua Nurse, Willean and Donald II Canty, my brother Jerry Wilson and my grandchildren, who are the epic center of my life story: Dru Anthony Gibson, Emory Gibson, Dante, Daryllis, Daryl Jr, Derrell and Darius Nurse.

I pray you all do not taste the sour grapes, but prosper and be blessed. May you learn all you can from my mistakes and life lessons from God above and receive all you need from your abilities, gifts, and talents. May your lives be filled with true love, joy, happiness, laughter, health, success, family, friendship, marriage, children, and grandchildren of your very own. Lastly, may faith sustain you when challenges of life evaluate you.

I want to honor my late parents, Clarice Bell, Joe Wilson, and my brother, Joseph Wilson. I am saddened you all did not live to see this book published. I pray you rest in peace and know my love is eternal.

Contents

Prologue

Trust yourself. You know more than you think you do.

—Benjamin Spock

Be who you are and say what you feel because those who mind don't matter and those who matter don't mind.

—Bernard Baruch

Instead, God chose the foolish things of the world to shame the wise; God chose the weak things of the world to shame the strong. God chose things despised by the world, things counted as nothing what the world considers important.

—1 Corinthians 1:27-28

I AM GETTING OLDER, AND life is getting shorter. I do not have too much time to live, so, I want the remainder to be my best—with intention and without regrets. I want my children and grandchildren to see me as a real person, not just a mother and grandmother. For safekeeping, I want to leave them with my thoughts, memories, fears, dreams, the history of who I am, and who my people are. But most of all, I want to pass what I have learned on to my children and grandchildren.

What matters most is speaking up, being generous, and inhabiting this life creating a new one. I want to explore what living really means. I hope to leave my loved ones with an instruction manual to guide them as they live their lives without me. This manual is not about where to buy groceries. Throughout this work, I will imitate how to treat people and themselves, how to love, what to stand up for, and what to care about. Time only seems to matter when it is running out. I always desired for my children to have the best, I just did not know it required more than giving material gifts.

My hustling cost me dearly. I did not have a clue that trying to be like my father and imitating people who have the best of both worlds. My father who I love dearly I tried hard to be like him in so many ways. As a young girl my father use to give me expensive jewelry, clothes, money and all that made me feel good. I realize most boys would like to be like their fathers, yet I was a little girl. I did not feel safe growing up as a little girl. I did not know my dad was committing crimes to care for his family. In all that we do for our children invest in their education ability and charisma. Sometimes I believe I was destined to have my life torn apart because it seemed like everything, I tried to do I end up failing at it. I desperately wanted people to recognize me. However, I did not know that recognition only comes from God. Instead, I of spending my youth as the person God wanted me to be I sat behind bars. I gained some wealth but lost something more precious in the process. I was not there for my children. I gave them much parenting as I could through visits, mail, phone calls and furloughs none of those could ever be enough. I see what I saw when my dad was out or in prison. We shared the same things in common. Little girls do not phantom anything at the age of five and six years old to determine anything of this nature. I know I was a inquisitee who always ask a lot of questions. They had better make sense to me as a child or else it would be hard for me to understand it if it looked a different way to me and more questions followed. This is how kids are especially smart kids. They always have questions for you. The more I perpetuated the consequences of my actions the more they haunted me. I created schemes and I was paid yet I paid with my life.

Whenever I used someone, I earned money and that was not good, nothing good comes from using anyone. My greatest fear was that I would fail my children. I believed hustling would keep my family comfortable. I was going in the wrong direction. I am now a survivor committed to change. My story permeates my past lifestyle.

To read without reflecting is like eating without digesting.

—Edmund Burke

Once, I was a young kid who grew up wanting so much to be like her dad. My younger self saw myself attracted to the beautiful and fine things in life the family couldn't afford. The older I became, the more my ways mirrored my dad's: hustling, stealing, and working hard. Both parents validated me as a special and visionary child, someone who would become great. My life changed irrevocably upon my incarceration. While on trial in federal court on three separate occasions, I won notoriety.

My sister saw me as a threat because both parents saw me as important, talented, gifted and bless. My sister lied about me in order to send me to prison so she could keep me out of our mothers will. Anything she would say to harm me would be damaging because I have a past. Something she have learned to use against me like others when they do not want you around. She was wise enough to say yes, she did it and this what she did without playing the blame game even if it were all true. Who else would inquire about a crime to put some money in their pocket, later inform the authorities? I am not thinking she would even consider such a thing, a gold mine, a plan to destroy me. Someone who is a narcissist not implementing themselves without being arrested. I would have not ever placed the blame on anyone never mine commit a crime to have someone tell on me. They all know I will not tell on them or myself. Today my eyes are open to what and how family use their family to harm them to get ahead, along looking out for oneself not considering who they hurt doing it. Even so much as my daughter who has committed crimes used my ID and anything she could get a hold of. The moment I would discover what she has done here comes the super big old threat something out of statute of limitation. She is trying to use it to comfort her ego against me. I now discovered more crimes, she committed using my info, easy access and I have a past being a felon. All lies anything one could say about me. The bs people and authorities do to harm people. There have been times being in prison my credit worthiness is being used being I have good credit. Who would use it? A family member not as much care how much they damage my credit. Even if they receive all they could receive in credit. We must be careful who we use in life because we all get our very own karma. I have used people to have what I want; wrong we do not use anyone at all. It all comes back some hundred-fold sometimes two. One may ask when does the agony stops?

While in prison, my dad passed away. The department of corrections forgot to put in my furlough papers to attend the funeral and view dad's body. While my dad was still at the funeral home, my sister's only child was there as well, two family members at same time. A horrible feeling. My nephew murdered during a robbery. Now, both my dad and nephew lay at Fuqua Funeral Home.

I had to emerge from the person I have been for the sake of my grand-kids. At age sixty, I resolutely pursues my goals and dreams in spite of a lifetime of challenges. I did not know how to get from one point to the other on my own. I made numerous attempts and had great ideas, but I needed more than just myself.

The devil tried to keep me at a standstill. I recently discovered it is the enemy who helps you reach your goals. I did not have a clue that the devil engaged in me being raped. I say this because when God has a plan and purpose for my life so does the enemy. After being raped I was filled with so much hate, rage, bitterness, and pain that I became a walking time bomb waiting to explode. At the age of fourteen where I suppose to be at the beach, camping and water skiing I really felt like nothing, a nobody. What it did to me, destroyed me. I were uncomfortable with young girls I knew would not become part of their lives who went to summer programs from wealthy surrounding towns where I always wanted to be part of, other than those from the hood. I did not feel in place at all when I attend school or when I did other things girls my age did. I just did not feel I belonged simply because of something someone done to me to have his way being an idiot. A pervert, a child molester, a rapist, someone who is sick. I have a confession to make the very person I love and respect my father I begin to develop a love hate relationship. He was to protect me. This is where I spent many years seeking out older men because I felt they would be my protector. I did not have a clue that even some of the older men who sought me were more than perverts themselves. I married a man who was thirteen years older than me. A man who even sought me out even when I was just fifteen years old, later became my husband. At that time, I did not even know he was a pervert. And this is where I begin to develop a suspicion with men.

When God anoints you, others attack to feel powerful. When a woman is great at what she does, she deserves to be on someone hit list. I was not anointed to be abandoned. Success is a threat to those around, not a disease from which an individual suffers. Never let people tell you that you cannot do something; their limitations are not yours. It does not mean you cannot do it.

I will be a different person. I will take the risk and do what I believe in. People only remember the extraordinary. As God did for me, God will turn you around and break the chains of your life. God heals whom He wants to heal and blesses whom He wants to bless. He touches whom He wants to touch. He called me. I heard and seen Him in action using me and I ran ignored Him and tried to put Him off. And He was yet there for me to see me no matter what age I am today. The older and wiser I get, to see who God has used for His glory in the Bible and out of the Bible. I find it amusing even with Moses. He was an older man by the chance he got it together. And it happened. God used me according to His purpose.

When I reflect on my transformation, I think of David emerging from the ranks to confront Goliath. Like him, I too split from my past habits, which proved to be my greatest adversary. This is something you do not understand until you see a revelation of it for yourself. I had to rethink my life and take my revelation to my personal Zion.

This is my last chance. I have erred too many times not to seize it. I am someone who has nothing to lose. Get out of my way because I have business for the Lord. God is a God of a first second third fourth and many chances. He is more than a second chance to me. I have done it repeatedly, in and out of prison too many times. He is a God who puts things all together again for me. I am a survivor of rape, sexual assault, prison, being abused by men, used by men and taken advantage of by people who seen goodness in me, and they are not comfortable with who they are, so they take advantage of the situation to destroy a friendship of blessings. This thing happens daily with people. I am careful who I have as a friend or acquaintance in my life today.

When choices have cost you, you are not easily pushed from your path.

Today, no devil in Hell will make me stray. Though he may bring disorders, dreams, business, visions, attitudes, dispositions, properties, or marriage, none of it will loosen my grip again. I have been through fire, flood, and trials.

Every age carries a new challenge. Experience taught me to be suspicious about life and most certainly men. Uncertainty made me cautious, and I underestimated men including my father. These men shared a lot of things in common such as untrustworthiness, life is not to be full of pain. Whereas fourteen-year-old girls are not to be raped. I have developed a pattern to where I would get you before you get me.

I did not realize I had demons on my back, a generational curse I must cast off. Pride must go because it is the only thing in God's way. God gives grace to the humble. To fear the Lord is to hate evil and arrogance. Prayer is intimacy with God, and when you do not pray, you talk to the devil. This is something I did not know. I heard about demons. I heard about praying but when you're filled with anger, rage, resentment, and bitterness how does one pray? I grew up in a Christian home. My mother was a Christian on fire for the Lord. She taken us to church, bible study, choir practice and fellowship. We were always proactive in the C.O.G.I.C. I heard about Jesus because of everything that has transpired in my life up to the age of fourteen I felt God had abandon me. I tried to look at how my mother and grandmother believed in Jesus. I believed I would end up trusting Him as they did so He would be my protector.

Christianity continued to elude me because at the age of fifteen I got pregnant and at the age of sixteen my baby was delivered. And at the age of nineteen I found myself in prison. It was like the scariest thing in the world being in the unknown. When hearing stories about things such as being bullied, being in forceful relationship, and being raped by inmates, it has one really thinking. How do I get pass this? I did not encounter these issues, none. Having to squat and spread your butt cheeks while women offices staring at you constantly as if you did something wrong. There in the federal prison camp the men officers would walk right into the shower open area while you are in the shower, look at you as you wash your body in the nude. I had this happen to me. He stood there watching me and it was sad. I could not believe what I was witnessing just arrived been there for about a few days. I'm nearly nine months pregnant with my last child. And there was nothing you could do because the bureau of prison hired mostly all men than women for this prison. These men enjoyed their jobs there. I was told by a woman officer woman did not apply for these jobs or stay long simply because of what they see of the men officer taking totally advantage of their job there boldly. This is a way for the men to constantly apply for the positions at the women prison, keeping the women officers away to have all the sex to themselves is taking advantage again of these helpless women. Seeing other young girls who you may have known or went to school with who you would not ever thought would be in prison are in prison. Some of us may have similar issues be the ones you may feel most comfortable. Then you bond with someone who's lonely. The first person they see that gives them some attention is the one they're now going out with in prison. I was never a follower nor did I wish to be accepted by anyone who felt awkward about being in my present. I have discovered because I walk alone and did not walk in cliques among insecure females, that did not like me for the least bit. The more I noticed this the more I knew many females were not my friend no matter what it was they may have asked of me. I have had conversations with myself concerning what I notice in other females they did not know their worth, having potential and yet not using it. Some of the females would just use people for whatever they could get soup, soap, toothpaste or anything. As for me I was always afraid of being involved with a female not to say none who did not like me. I was terribly afraid. I sometimes would blush seeing how women looked at me. I thought it was just a sex thing nothing more. It was something the church did not permit as I were growing up. The pastors preached about it in the pulpit as if it was such a filthy thing. We all get to our own level in spirituality. We all come to realization of who we going to be. I'm more open today I see life different. I am not blindsided by people or love we make choices good or bad. We all have problems. There is no one without problems but God. He created everything good and bad to work together for the good for those who love Him. Everyone needs love. God is love. And it sure goes a long way. Love plays many factors in everything, not just sexual. Many people are in relationships for many reasons and love do not always play any part of any of it. As a female I knew how I were basically what I wanted and what I did not. What I may do and what I will not. The average female looked at me as being a square. This is how the stage was set. If one acted like a square, you were able to see who's who. The real the fake and the haters. Being in relationships in prison was not safe or healthy. It was something I did not do. I knew it was something the church did not permit as I were growing up. Being more open today I see life totally differently. I am not blindsided by people or love.

I will not find my place until I find my purpose. I must break my own rules by doing something I've never done before—I need to change my attitude. I need to cast away how I once saw myself. This is a change God demands from me. My miracle is my discomfort. My withered hands need healing. After all I have been through, I must understand all God has for me. There is another person in me the world has not seen yet.

All my stories are similar to ones in the Bible. My stories occurred the way they did for God's purpose, for nothing happens without reason. One cannot place a seed into a closed womb. My miracle is not in what I lost, but in what is left. I still have time to become a new person and share my knowledge.

I had to escape the gravity of my past, a process proving to a life-long one. My struggles are the pathways to success, something had to die to balance my failures. Have you ever accessed what is in your hand—your ability to transform your own life? My blessing is hidden in my hand. Why does it take so many years to realize this truth? I had a limited perception of it. Now, I understand I can do more than I think I can do. I can have more than what I think I can have.

Scared and intimidated, I had to access the transformative ability at my fingertips. This problem was not coming from anyone but myself. No matter how I erred, I haven't reached the point where God will just allow for me to fall from His grace. I know He will bless people who make mistakes. God will aid you even when it is your mistake. He will fix problems for you. The power of life and death is in God.

I am no longer the person whom others knew. I was handpicked from my mother's womb. God reveals himself to redeem the lost and broken. The enemy's job is to keep me skeptical of the prophetic. The enemy knows God's plan and his greatest power is in making you doubt it.

Whenever God sends a prophet into your midst, it is for a purpose. To overcome doubt, I had to change what I say to myself and about myself. You need to believe in the Lord our God, so you will be established. If you want to prosper, you must believe His prophets.

I discovered, whenever God is doing something in my life, He changes the people around me. The seasons in your life are connected to the people in it, so you know your season has changed when your company has changed. If you're hanging around the same people, you're in the same season. There are those who only try to hang around to reap your cloak of blessings, being that you are a cheerful giver, believing they would always have their way of being blessed by you. These are those who are leeches. I have discovered who they are who were acquainted to me. These folks know I know who they are and try to yet hang on as a bee to a hive. I have learned to let them go do not care to have anything to do with them. Those same funds I noticed I gave out to them are funds I could have invested into stock a savings or some sort of investment. They just are not worthy of anything. Whenever God changes your season He changes whom you are connected to knowing not everyone can manage where God is ready to take you.

God hates anyone who takes advantage of your weakness. The devil, meanwhile, studies your childhood. It does not fight the grownup me, but where I am most vulnerable—the little kid. I now have a grip on it. My vulnerability is something God wants me to have in my hand. I acknowledge I did not have a grip on it in the past. Complacency perpetuated the devil's power in my life. I want it and hell to know—including my enemies, detractors, resistors, and haters—I got a grip on it. The enemy had to scare me for this to happen, but I did it. There are haters waiting on one mistake from me. My resiliency now withstands my self-doubt. In all of us, there is a pessimist, a doubter, an antagonist, and a sinner.

Do not judge people because they are flawed. Their flaw might be your perfection. Two people with problems can help one another if they do not have the same problem. One does not have to be without blemish to be my friend, but to be my friend is to let me do what I do. We must support one another. I have no tolerance for people intolerant of weakness.

I must use what I have. I have no tools this time. I must do what I have never done. My circumstances rise against me. I cannot worry about them; this is how I lost my grip. I must stop procrastinating and cut through the rock. God is going to support me. This is how you know you are anointed— when you can take less and do more with it.

My children remember me as a woman in and out of prison. I did not know who they are becoming as adults. My children in all the world are the most important to me. I devoted enormous energy to my life of crime. I believed I had to continue what I did to stay afloat. I never expected to be arrested and sent to prison.

Seeing my life as a story allows me to use a GPS-like road map to get from one point to another. When I need to make decisions, the GPS makes it clear and directs me. In the past, I never once had access to or any thoughts about navigating this way. It is all new to me. Sometimes I am lost. I sit and wonder how I got to one point and not the other.

Since I have problems, I need God. Through Him, I have finally taken the bold step of abandoning the lifestyle that kept me mired. I've been arrested and convicted too many times. I have forty forties and three misdemeanors. I did not go to prison each time. In many instances, a conviction consisted of ending the case with a fine, probation, restitution, incarceration, or a suspended sentence.

God gave me a purpose. I will not forget it with my vision, dreams and hope I will hold on until the end. My purpose shows me I can do all things through Christ, who lends me strength. Faith is my power to endure, and I choose not to sink.

I do what I do for my loved ones moves me to assume this extraordinary risk and responsibility. I am working hard to get it right and done to perfection.

There were people who told a lie on me just to have me arrested. The Judicial system plays a dirty game, and everyone knows how to play it even the lame. Some wrote false statements in the hope I would just plead out in court, but I have never pled out because I were afraid, only in the case of my sister a few years ago because I were on no nonsense probation. I had been told if I decide to not accept the plea offer and go to trial, they could give me forty years. Someone with a lengthy criminal background is how dirty the judicial system plays. We read, hear, and see how the FBI dept of justice, the justice department our law of the land high judges, prosecutors and people who are white supremacist who placed the blame on the ones least likely to succeed accusing those. This is what these folks been doing for generations. This is something that is pass down and will always repeat in history. Who would want to take a chance such as this seeing how they treat us Black people? I was not going to go against the system knowing the criminal justice system would do anything to place me behind the walls and not white Americans. Whenever I went to trial, I learned whom they were using and what they were saying against me.

I spent many years wondering why others lied on me. One person may tell a lie because she's unhappy or just doesn't like me. Sometimes, you leave a negative impression on others who do not know you, and because they are as foolish as the liar, they believe the latter. And there are the haters—they are those who worry, watch you, and are mad about who God created you to be. These are the folks who know you're God-chosen. The devil always knows what God has in store for His people.

Just because someone wrote a statement does not mean it will convict you. It only means you must spend unnecessary money and time to get out of the mess. It is about the court proving beyond a reasonable doubt you're guilty of the crime.

Criminal life, in the beginning, was intriguing, competitive, and challenging. There were young girls my age and older who were committing crimes but doing so on a much lower scale. And then there were girls who envied what I had. By keeping themselves in the proximity of talent, skill, or trade, they cloaked themselves in blessings. Otherwise, nothing going for them just plain scared. They would lean on a drug dealer for help. When caught, they would run their mouths to the authorities, yet I would not get arrested for it. I would totally deny their accusations and look them in the eyes without clenching my fists. There were moments I was able to lean on and trust Christ. However, I was not always able to avoid their lies, and I was stuck paying the consequences.

The importance of understanding my story is to see how it shaped me to create a new one. I feel connected with my life purpose and have more clarity on my mission in life. I no longer tolerate behaviors I should not have despite the toll on my self-respect. For the first time, I embrace the full concept of feeling empowered by learning about myself. It was something I was running away from my entire life.

I was a young girl who desired to grow up to be like her father. My father broke my heart when he went to prison. The tragedy was that my father did not know how to be a father, or to act as a father. I would observe my dad, me being a kid something I noticed as a child. He was afraid of discipling us and this was something we needed. He loved his kids. Dad left home to work for himself later married mom young. They were teenagers..

When he finally got out of prison, it was too late for he and I—there was no relationship between us. I felt betrayed because I blamed my dad for my incarceration. The more I learned about I am the blame for myself and make conscious decisions I will not blame no one for my mistakes. I was not in foster care or any of that stuff. My parents worked hard to provide for our family. I am learning to stop that cycle for the sake of my children and grandchildren.

I thought, whenever I started anew with God—whenever I bowed with repentance in prison—I was still missing something. A sinking feeling lingered. I refused to apply this repentance to a true direction. Studying God's word, I thought there must be something I was missing because every few years, I would stumble, slide, and fall once again. I know with all the abilities, gifts, talents, and skills He has given me, He will also impart His wisdom, knowledge, and understanding if I ask for it. At the time, I was not using those abilities for His purpose. I was constantly using them for selfish gain.

I began talking and praying to God I realized I still had not fulfilled my dream. At one point in my life, because of my ignorance, I stopped praying. I needed to know how life really worked and what I were living for.

Where was I in life? We all have a blind spot it continued to show up in my life. I did not have the right perspective. I never even noticed it. All my happiness was being delayed, postponed, or denied, but I was doing it to myself. I was always looking back, clinging to the pitfalls of stupidity.

I was constantly thinking more on what had happened than what will happen. My eyes were fixed on the rearview mirror of life, and so I crashed each time. I spent so long looking back in fear. What was I afraid of?

We must trust in God whatever the future holds He will enable us to manage it when the time comes. Wherever we are going God has already been there to pave the way. When we fear going through something God gives us strength.

When I think back over the mess, I put myself through I ask myself how I emerged from it? The answer is because of His grace, mercy, and power. This is something I am not deserving of or worthy of because of what I have done, something so horrible that I could not turn from my wicked ways and be obedient to His will was such a hassle for me during times. He enabled me to do what I needed to do. He brought me through difficulty so many times. We may not know the future, but by knowing the One who holds the future in His hands, we can look forward without fear. If God brings you a challenge, He will carry you through it.

Come to Him and ask for wise, not foolish, things. God has promised to contend with what challenges me when I'm living right. He is steadfastly concerned about my life. Always remember, the devil will try to sabotage you. My plan remains with God.

I recognize my errors. I am trying another way until I learn to live for my purpose. When I reflect on my life, I think of all the wasted time. But that lost time only means there was something else for me to learn. I am working on building new habits. Only by practicing over and over will I make them natural. Learning is about making mistakes until my subconscious mind puts together the right picture. No matter how long I was not doing what was right, I can still create a new pattern. I am planting the seeds of success, and they will grow into an abundant harvest.

Before, I did not make any changes because I was not aware of my wounded childhood. I disassociated myself from it. I did not realize my trauma came from the shadows of correctional officers beating the living shit out of a young woman in shackles. They beat others who were pregnant and unable to defend themselves, too. I also lived on a housing tier with someone who hung herself, and months later it happened again. I watched while they tried reviving the body, although she was already dead. It is so unfair and unconstitutional to abuse anyone physically like the correctional officers do in the women facility at York Correctional Institute.

The officers have sex with women and young girls, some who are mentally ill. I have seen the officers in state and even federal facilities violate inmates without remorse. The more, they spoke of the situation as if it were a joke.

These officers are not just single men isolated from personal relationships—they had wives and girlfriends. These COs are diabolical not caring cruel. They take advantage of us who are powerless. They do not have any heart. We continue to go back and forth to prison knowing the same things exist there. We see what goes down in prison and nothing changes. The administration is aware of these situations, and nothing seems to change. As for those who do not have any power continue to be used, abuse, manipulated and deceived. It seems that everybody is looking for a way to get over and get by. There have been times I seen girls doing things they had no business doing but they did it just to get by. Some did not even have commissary to get by, forget the indigent money of $5.00 the prison gives you once a month to be able to get one soap and toothpaste or use it for stamps. There are some who do not even have family in their lives, so they allow these diabolical COs to do what they want to them. These are females who walk around as if their shit does not stink because they have favor with these low life officers feeling they are better only better off in prison. And these COs do not have any remorse for what they do to them. These girls commit suicide. These girls go through pure hell. And people wonder why do you go back to prison? I do not know why I continued to go back other than the mere fact material things turn me on. This stuff make me feel good. And to feel good I must go back into a tough situation, come out and go right back into an unpleasant situation again. The ball is closing in on me, not only counts but countless shake downs, where we must stand bend over and spread your cheeks men and women officers degrading you and no one seems to care from the commissioner all the way down to the Cos. These guys are diabolic devilish. They have no heart. They do not care. And this is what prison is about. The walls continue to close in on you day and night and there is nothing you could do about it. As for some people just join and become part of the game. It is a way of survival sometimes. You must be strong to say no I am not doing that I am not doing that. Quite naturally you're not going to get any favors. One must stand on what you know and believe in your moral's values and principles. Then you have Co's in your life determining if you should go home or not, being they're in charge. These Co's have the mighty pen to write down on a piece of paper anything on you and you have no way of proving what they say is wrong to get a guilty verdict on you. Seventy percent is part of the recidivism rate. Those of us who returns to prison wear our shame and guilt. There are some who no longer wear it only to find themselves in an awkward situation this happens. We find ourselves programming harder than ever learning more discovering something new in ourselves. Now later be able to hold our head up high not because we are being released but we learned something differently about ourselves. I have seen officers and counselors marry inmates, resign from their jobs and some retire just to be with an inmate. But when these officers are get investigated by the feds or tasks force by the state, arrested and convicted they receive a lifetime as their sentence more than the state gives. I have seen state officers keep their jobs and just transfer to another facility. This consequence is inconvenient at worst- their new location may be further to travel or may be locked down twenty-four hours a day in a facility with the inmates. State officers are more shielded, especially if they serve several years and know someone in high rank. It benefits them to be labeled a "good officer".

In the state I would see predatory officers escorted to protective custody. The same occurs with enlistees who assault and abuse young girls. They violate women and are quickly transferred. Their lives go on. It becomes the norm for them; assault, move and assault again. For the women, life freezes. When you thought it was over, the traumatic experience permeates one's life without her knowledge. This abuse continues as a mental battle when no one have received the proper therapy treatment. One would go into the prison system recovery takes vulnerability- one needs to talk about it. She than need to find herself, with grace and power.

You could move from pain to power by reeducating yourself. The Bible refers to this process as renewing your mind. We must learn to think differently. If we been taught to fear, we can also be taught to be confident, courageous and bold. We must not allow fear to stymie our success or joy in life.

We all have weaknesses and imperfections- whether it is in our relationships or in our finances. Most of the time we deny, hide, or defend our faults. God permitted them deliberately in my life to demonstrate His power through me. God uses imperfect people to do extraordinary things despite their weaknesses- that is, a limitation we all inherit and have no power to change.

Sometimes that limitation might be a disability, a handicap, a chronic illness, yet it can also be a hurtful memory, a personality trait, or even a talent. There is no one who is not flawed, except Jesus. For years, I thought I could not be saved, for I believed God could not use me after I fell.

When I first accepted Christ into my life at the age twelve. I knew upon accepting Him I would desire all He has for me and would never leave Him.

I was not thinking I could do this all alone at all. Then at nineteen years old I again surrendered to Christ. I found myself in my very own mess. I needed Jesus to use me. I did not think it was not happening as I could see in my life, yet I was winning souls to Christ and did not know any of what I was looking for. All I did was cry when I was all alone talking to God saying I would not do this again attend church, Bible study and choir practice everything I knew to do growing up. God, however, is never limited by our limitations. The Bible says," We are like glass-fragile and prone to break into pieces. In prison at nineteen years old someone who refused to listen. The very moment I would be release I stay the course until I find myself doing something wrong again getting myself into trouble again. I notice this in so many patterns and now feeling it more so than ever. What is it Lord I'm not getting Jesus? The more I discover myself learning more of who God is and how badly I need Him. I realize that I must find myself and find myself a church that is not afraid of learning and speaking the truth. What I remember growing up in my family church is how relatives told lies or constantly talked about one another in quiet, those who did not attend church or if you did attend church they forgot about their devilish children, whorish husbands and themselves. Yet they talked about you and yours. Once you heard their take and seen them again you did not wish to partake or even fellowship with them anymore. When it happens one time you forgive. When it happens again you try to forgive learn about forgiveness forgive them sincerely and move on without them. These are the people who been in the church their entire life and knows nothing about who God is. They do not see themselves or know anything about their issues. They have the worst problems.

My recovery from crime gave life to my religion. It taught me to live in faith every day. My spirituality stems from my individual and collective experiences. My experiences, moment to moment, bring value to my spirituality. During some point in my life, I lost my sense of spirituality. Yet my past and present experiences give me a chance to rediscover it. The challenge in this post-transformation part of my evolution is to learn about myself intensely but to also commit myself to the considerable task of dealing with the good and the bad, the discoveries, and the setbacks. I'm giving myself everything I am capable of because I'm now capable of it. I saw common elements necessary to create an impressive person no matter what I did. I have uncovered a set of practices, principles, and beliefs necessary for success no matter what my goals are in life. God is able to do more than I would ever dare to ask or even dream of infinitely beyond my highest prayers, desires, thoughts, or hopes. Resentment beat me daily, and one morning, I awoke with the realization that animosity was like a garment I wore. I was only hurting myself, and with the change came revelations. When I was well again, resentment never again crossed my mind.

Life is a test. My perspective has influenced how I invest my time, use my talents, and value my relationships. It is important to understand how you see your life. It is a game of cards—you must play the hand you are dealt. The Bible offers three metaphors: life is a test, life is a trust, and life is a temporary assignment. God evaluates people's character, faith, obedience, love, integrity, and loyalty. Words such as trial, temptation, and test occur more than two hundred times in the Bible. Every time you pass a test, God notices and plans to reward you in eternity. Money is both a test and a trust from God. When we flirt with the temptations of this world, God calls it spiritual adultery—you are cheating on Him. It is our responsibility to learn to love God because God is love. If all you want is your own way, you become His enemy.

My Birth and Childhood

"Who are you?" someone asks. "I am the story of myself,"
comes the answer.

—M. Scott Momaday

I AM NO ACCIDENT. MY parents' DNA, their sins—everything about them speaks to God's plan for me.

As a child, I did not know it took many steps to realize one's purpose in Christ. The moment I accepted Him as my Lord and Savior, I expected Him to be with me all the days of my life. And yes, He was, but not in the way I expected. I had to embody this truth for myself and trust Him, even when I felt alone.

The church I grew up did more preaching than teaching. I have learned through life teaching is vital. There are things we just do not know; we think we do. Some pastors are not knowledgeable in what it is their preaching to you. It may sound good to your ears you ask yourself is it correct? Who are you following? There are some who have not ever gone to Ministry school to study the Bible to know anything. The church has been passed down to them and this is all they know collecting offerings and tithes. Some who truly see that it's not a bad thing what God has for you to do. Do we do it or procrastinate? Then you have some who are mad at their pastors who go start a church just to get back clueless to what they're doing just to say they have a store front church. We may have all started out in store fronts, yet God has opened doors for them to have mega churches or something much bigger than they had. Before I forget we also know there are some who do believe they're perfect. What they're preaching is solely for the congregation not for themselves. As for me I enjoy when pastors include themselves to their preaching. It shows he has nothing to hide. This is a big deal and real. I do know they're not going to tell it all. That's if unless you hear something about them in the media. I am not bashing anyone. I love God's people. We must be willing to see a revelation as were reading the Bible. This is for us all who we allow to feed us God's Word. God wants me to use my experience to help others drowning in the same waters.

Through it all, God's grace has carried me. My purpose here—my life—is far greater than my personal aspirations. My own hedonism and attitudes were a pride rendered visible only with time. Convictions, convictions, and more convictions took the wheel and drove me down a path lined with bars. I had no idea where my life was headed. Everything I ever wanted for myself has cost others and me. I believed, to get what I needed and wanted, I could only do so at the expense of someone else. The things I did were for the wrong reasons. I did not include my Creator in any of it. Although subconsciously aware of the consequences of my actions, I ignored them as if I were blind. I did not understand why because I was busy and without purpose. My short-term thinking was not good enough for my God. He desired all of me, and I knew it.

Growing up, my father excelled at providing for us. He financially took care of his kids, except when he was incarcerated. And even so much inside the prison where my dad was, he sent home large sums of money only to send it back into the prison for things for himself, much to my dismay, his life revolved around cheating, which was how he supplemented his income. My dad's only conception of how to earn money came from his own upbringing. As an adult, he did not educate himself, either in prison or out. Everything my dad did for us, he meant for our benefit. He gave to his kids in abundance.

Whenever he came around—which, when he was not in prison, was often—we always received three hundred dollars each and more if he came around. We would go shopping and buy what we needed. He would bring us to his home, where he lived with a woman older than my mother. She was a nurse who owned horses and an extravagantly large house. My dad had few various sources of income; in one capacity, he drove modular homes to their sites. In another, he was a gambler, but not at a casino. He did his gambling with Italians, who made their money from people-gambling. They called *bookies*.

Sometimes, while I waited for the bus to bring my siblings and me to camp, I would go to their shop to buy candy. The shop had a section where they sold cigarettes, cigars, soda, and sweets. They even had State Line chips—my favorite. This was not an average candy store. The guys in this store were old white men, who smoked cigars and stood around talking. They kept regular business hours; the place had been around for a decade. A few years ago, the town tore down the building. Most of the historic buildings in the area were yet abandoned.

My mother did all the demanding work of caring for the four of us—doctor appointments, PTA meetings, choir practice, church, fishing, shopping, and preparing our meals. My father, on the other hand, would always bring my siblings and me to visit Boston. When we were out of school for the summer and holidays, we would visit our grandparents and relatives. He was one of eleven children, and all his siblings also had children. Whenever we visited, we were always busy doing fun things together, watched movies at the movie theater went shopping, baking was a favorite. We dressed up in little girl toy heels and tiara princess crowns. This is how we saw ourselves. We filled each day with kite flying and playing with the chemistry toys my brother Joey always used.

My paternal grandmother, Grandma Honeycomb, was an articulate cook. Her meals were gut busting. My grandmother would always ask where's mother—Candy, she called her, because of my mom's penchant for sweet potato and peach cobblers—did not come with us. Mother would call Grandma to send her love, but she never visited. I am certain Grandma Honeycomb knew my dad was the reason.

Witty and sharply discerning, my mom knew my dad was a womanizer. Yet, she chose not to confront him. I'm sure when mom discovered my dad was unfaithful, she consummately let him go. After they separated, she seemed happy to live singly with us. She liked her mother and sister's company, and she got along well with her neighbors. Mom, she never had a circle of women friends. I never heard my parents fight or argue, and there was never any abuse or any loud noise. My mother was content and easygoing. I loved being with her as well.

On Saturdays, my mom went to garage sales, rummage sales, and auctions with her mother and sister. I would go everywhere with them. I loved seeing all the beautiful things for sale, eating the grilled hotdogs and drinking a Coke at the auctions. In long lines at rummage sales, we would buy coffee and donuts early morning to get the best picks of the crops. They were good at getting impressive bargains on antique items, and I have learned to value and adore antiques. Mom would always give some of her best antiques to her brother, Lewis, who owned his own antique business. He was a welder and did marvelous work on all his pieces that may have needed some work.

My siblings were much older than I. We all hung out with totally different people did different things were all still a close-knit family. If I ever had problems with anyone, I could always tell my brothers. They were loving, good young men, not troublemakers.

My brother Joey, the second child, was incredibly intelligent. He was a well-rounded guy with a multitude of talents and always got the job done. Plus, he was always there for my family. He was more like our mother than our father with all the caretaking he did. Otherwise, he kept mostly to himself, even growing up. He knew people, yet he was a homebody. He later got married and had kids. Joey was my hero.

He passed away young—only forty years old. We all mourned Joey. After twenty years, I still do.

Knuckie, my sister, is the eldest of us. My mom said when she was five years old, a car hit her, and she was pronounced dead. My mother cried and begged God for Knuckie's life. Her cries prevailed. God spared Knuckie. We as parents and mothers knows what it could be like if put in a certain situation such as a child's life is at stake never expecting any such thing as this to happen not to my child. We may wear diverse types of hats during the time hats of grief, assault, murder, forgiveness and the unknown. We as people never know until we are placed in a situation such as. Growing up, my sister was never home. She attended church conventions with our grandma, where there were always children her age and of her faith. Often, she dated. When she and her boyfriend were not in fellowship, they ran away from home many times. Mom and my paternal grandmother spoke over the phone, and when they found Knuckie's whereabouts, they both pick the pair up and return them back home. She and her boyfriend were always found in New Haven. It happened so many times, both sets of parents decided they should get married. And they did.

Knuckie had a baby boy. She named him after his dad: her husband, Charles. We called Charles "Dudie". Eventually, I had to go live with them. Her husband worked and my sister needed help with the baby, mom said. I was a teenager by then, and I was an immense help to my sister.

Mann was my baby. He named after his dad Charles but Mann for his nickname. He was a precious baby and a fine baby. I was a kid caring for a baby who loved his auntie. I cared for him as an adult would have. I bathed him, dressed him fed him and put him to bed. He had the sweetest smile with his curly thick hair. We also spent quality time together teaching him to count, his ABC's and watched educational movies Barney. I spent most of my teen years caring for my nephew. There was only one other person who would come and pick up Mann: his grandmother father's mother. It's her oldest son who is now married with a wife and baby. The entire family excited. She bought Mann savings bonds regularly, clothing and did fun things at amusement parks together. Mom saw to it Mann attended the best schools hung around good kids and brought him to church with her. She was Mann's other mom. He began to call her his Ma as a child.

My brother Jerry accused of two armed robberies the authorities could not make a case against him lacking evidence, no one to cosign for five years. The same week statute of limitations was due to close two common informants known for their petty shoplifting was arrested needed to get out on bond. They both Mark Williams and a close family friend gave up information they heard. It's always this format family friend. The authorities taken a fourteen-page statement they wrote for them to sign. It happens.

Jerry would give his last to anyone, but he enjoyed watching lots of TV shows with police officer's cowboy and Indians with guns. The Wild West was one of Jerry's favorite tv shows. He would practice drawing a gun he never had until he learned to draw his very own gun. We as parents should always prevent our kids from playing robbers or playing with any toy gun. This is a no-no, people. He has always taken things into his own hands. It's sad—now, I see many of his actions came from neglect from both our parents. There were no foster parents in our lives to pick up the pieces of nurturing, educating, and giving us the love, we needed to grow. Our grandmother watched us while mom worked long hours and we did things such as soliciting a building fund for our church home, fishing, amusement parks, and attend camps. Sometimes this is not enough when parents do not know what to do to be a parent as far as educating their children because their parents did not know how to educate them. So now with their own they do not know or understand how to do it for their own. It becomes a pattern that follows on in the generations to come until someone decide to do it differently and break the curse by educating themselves in unusual ways. I do not want to blame our parents because they only did the best they knew how to. Others can turn their eyes and blame anyone they choose to, but today, I know differently. People have always taken Jerry's kindness for granted and taken advantage of him, just as you would. Even I would. Like people has taken advantage of you and me. If he was there to help someone, then everything was all right.

I remember being a young kid—seven or eight years old. Jerry was eleven or twelve at the oldest. A former boxing manager asked Jerry to kill someone for five hundred dollars. In the sixties, five hundred dollars was a lot of money. But to kill someone? Not enough. No way. My brother often helped kids and parents at the neighborhood gym. One day, they did not need him, so he went home. The man came to our house, looking for him. Teenagers, malleable, can be manipulated into committing crimes.

The man knocked, since in the projects we did not have doorbells. Mom answered the door, invited him in, and sent for Jerry. She knew who this man was, but he never once came inside to pick up my brother. Jerry always walked in the projects. But that day, he and Mr. Dukes left our home. Upon Jerry's return, he removed his jacket, and mom asked,

"So, what did Mr. Dukes want with you that he came to get you for?"

Jerry did not expect the question from Mom, but as if it were nothing, he told her, "He wanted me to kill someone for him for five hundred dollars."

My mother reeled. "You will do no such thing. What he asked you to do is wrong. You can go to jail for that. The man must be crazy."

I am certain when Mr. Dukes saw Jerry the next day, he questioned him about any suspicion from Mom. None of the man's plans materialized.

Afraid for our safety, we moved from Bellevue Square housing project to a garden-style apartment on the other side of town. It might have been safer. At least we hoped my brother would not be solicited to kill a stranger over five hundred dollars in the new neighborhood.

Me, meanwhile—a young kid going into fourth grade—missed my Bellevue Square friends so much, I cried every day. I thought I would never see Georgia or her sisters again. Georgia and her sister's parents only allowed for me to come in to play with them when their parents were not home. We played as little girls would play jump rope, hopscotch and maybe allowed others to play in our hair. We had fun there at their house. They did have brothers who did boy things among themselves. I did not know we would ever see one another ever in life. A few years went by Cynt and I would begin to have fifty cent parties, where all the gang bangers would come to see Cynt and I who may wanted to dance with being beautiful young girls. During our first party I did not know I would now begin to see Georgia who attended our parties a few times with the rest of her girlfriends. These girls would be able to walk from one project to other projects without being jumped or afraid. These young girls always had one another's back. The young guys never caused any problems never any fights. When our parties would be over, everyone enjoyed themselves. These young men came with Stacy Adams shoes, Stetson and Kango hats and cashmere coats no more than twelve thirteen and fourteen years old. They were hustling all their lives. This was a way for their escape when no one was there to guide them and myself. There were some who wore their gang banging jacket with their logos to our party. Gangs then in my era of the 60's -70'-magnificent twenties, the hustlers were young men who all stuck together who may have been caught out as I was for some. Our management staff did not mind allowing for Cynt and I to give parties in our basement. We sold sodas for fifty cents and played good music with a red or black light bulb. All the girls who I may have known from the Bellevue Square always got their dance in with whomever they liked; this was sufficient.

However, I did not want to leave any of my friends behind. As it turned out, I soon made friends with a girl, Cynt, who would become my childhood BFF. Her first cousin had a crush on me, and we began to talk on the phone at nine years old.

At the time, a season of developmental creativity abounded inside me. Although the person I would become remained unclear, I began stepping in an uncertain direction.

Early into my young adult life, I did not have many romantic relationships. There was one man with whom I was vulnerable, though: Buno. I believed everything he said to me. Crazy, right? During that time, I never imagined him being my husband. He was married when we met. I was going through my divorce myself. He asked me to draft up his divorce decree. I did without any hesitation faxed a copy to her. I did it because this man just wanted out of his marriage. She thought she would scare him by filing for a separation knowing he had his mind made up. As for her she needed financial support. This was about to end, and she knew it. He also was not in love with her anymore, which she knew. I would not play any games with her or any man and at that point in my life. She was heated about me being older and he six years younger than I. He saw something attractive in me and wanted to leave his family. He told me he was not happy and felt the need to move on. This was something she had decided to try to hold me to the cross with. It was not happening at all. He had married young against his wishes. He claimed he only did it because his mom said it was the right thing to do when he got his girlfriend pregnant. He spent sixteen thousand on his wedding and was with her for about nine years before he met me.

Buno had a black art business, a drug dealer and a homeowner. Although he sold drugs someone who hustled but not a hustler. He felt comfortable with someone who produced more than he to keep himself afloat ahead of the game without being swallowed up. Not everyone who is out there in the street doing wrong is a hustler. Sometimes the small is enough for some. He spent his money wisely and cared for whomever he needed to – his five kids, me and his mortgage. I made sure he had a nine to five. He wanted to be able to work with his firearm not being in the street yet being productive. He had a entirely different mindset with an older woman in his life. He was truly amazed when we begin to date. Everything was different and new for him. I was like to him his mother being a mom's boy. Someone who did not wish to undo my hand from his. I adored him as much as he admired me. I saw what a great dad he was with his kids. All I could do was give him some babies. It was the most I gave –not my hand in marriage. There is no excuse when a man cheats on his significant other her will not cheat on you. He being younger not a lot of experience I knew he was not ready for total commitment. I was right. Did I side with him about his behavior? Nah. I am a firm believer that what a man does to other women he will do to you. I feared this. I would not turn my eyes to it. The more we discussed it the more he hurled excuses. As for me you can use an excuse one time only.

During this period, I was in federal court, trial after trial. I knew the government wanted to send me to prison. Buno came into my life during the third of six years awaiting trial. I needed someone to be there for me one hundred and fifty percent and he was not, yet a little boy. I had two homes, a range rover, funds in the bank, a millinery unisex retail store, three young children and a teenager just entering first year in college. I wanted my man and family to relocate to where I was being housed at the prison camp in West Virginia. This was something he did not do or ever considered so I knew it was not for him. He liked what I had to show. A beautiful lovely lady with young children I cared for, two homes, business happy and funny.

As for Buno everything I had tempted him. As a matter of fact, when I was sentenced to prison, he moved out of our home. He moved with his new girlfriend he than married. She was so afraid I would interfere in their lives nothing I did, I thought about it, too much of a hassle. There were other females who had the opportunity to do what she expected me to do which I knew. Their lives were living hell. Yet they did not wish to have anyone know what was going on other than my children.

Buno had taken my kitchen appliances and my three-piece, ten-thousand dollars bedroom set, which he claimed he taken for our son or daughter to sleep in. I would not allow another woman's furniture in my home, let alone bedroom furniture on which my man and I slept unless I did not know. He had her in our home we shared together. My oldest daughter would tell me Fe-Fe did her hair. I could not figure out who was Fe-Fe sound like a pet name as a dog, yet it was, she his female he was dating. As a womanizer, he did not know how to nourish a woman's needs. I had to teach him a few things from the bedroom. He was one hundred percent a cheater, his truth endured despite our support for one another.

I feared for myself something you know is wrong you do it anyway not caring what the percussions would be. We sometimes do this not caring at all and it comes back to bite us in the face. Then you have others who did the same thing you did yet will hang onto dear life accepting all the bs with him being a whoremonger and hope no one knows their marriage is on a whim. They both stay holding onto what they could get from one another and that is misery. He was respectful and afraid of allowing me to know any of his dirt being a common drug dealer. They like to sling in the bedroom, hotel, car anywhere if you know what I mean. Yet his tendencies were enough for me to accept what I needed to do. This was not my plan for a future with someone. I was not ready, being six years older than him and knew better. In retrospect, I know my heart was correct in how I imagined his thoughts of me, "let me get her now thought".

We both lied and kept secrets. We said things to each other because we knew it was what the other person wanted to hear. I may have said those things because I did not have enough strength or courage to tell the truth. "I just wanted you for a season and a reason". He was getting money and had assets. He had too many young children by too many women some were messy except his second daughter mom who were respectful and had her own life. Whatever the case, I needed his acceptance. It was easy for me to lie to him and myself. I am not that woman today.

As children and people of God, we pass through trials. We are connected to God like a branch on a vine being the branch bearing fruit. The branch He also trims. Apart from Him we can do nothing. If anyone does not remain in Christ. He is like a branch that is thrown away and withers such branches are picked up and thrown into the fire and burned. In this process, you lose progress. As a child of God, you must have faith in your mind and heart He will replace what He cuts with something better. I expect God to return what the cankerworm, the locust, and palmerworm have taken from me. For God to do something new in my life, old habits, relationships, and circumstances must erode. I now know I'm savvy, cagey, beautiful, Lovin, funny and fun. I squandered many years pretending. The husband I believed I always desired from God: He has given me. A spiritual God-fearing loving man who under-stands me and I understand him. This being my heart desire all my life wanting a spiritual God-fearing all-knowing man of God. I understand there is nothing easy and we all have some good and bad. I can say this has been all I needed in my life, and I finally have it. Sometimes it takes the opposite of someone to help one another in the area of life that easily beset someone. I must always look to God in every way even when I do not feel I do not want too. This is something

I must do regardless of anything. God is doing something differently in me for me and through me to toughen me for His purpose. We have both decided and understand this is for duration. We do not have the time and energy to get ourselves involved in other relationships of something we both have done in our past. We did not just lust over one another or become infatuated, of one another but decided this is the one for me good or bad in GOD we trust. I am not that woman today to not be certain if this is something I would want or not. There comes a time in life you get older wiser and smarter to know this is your last rodeo do it right or leave it alone it's for you or not. I no longer look for the external approval or validity of who I am from others. The feelings of inadequacy I learned as a child transposed into my adulthood life, and yet I sutured on a smile and thought none would be the wiser. I wanted to be this person everyone loved and befriended. I squandered embodying my truth for people I did not even trust. When I knew someone was not right for me, I accepted it. They were leeches from the grave without remorse.

What do you do when you feel like you are running out of time? Everything I ever envisioned as possible I must challenge. I must stretch every muscle, endure possibilities for myself, utilize my resources, skills to turn things around for the good of my legacy, and for my grandkids. Why feel empowered when you know you have the power to do anything through Christ? So, in my stories, what I experienced is not a loss, but a win. My hurdles encourage those who face the same strife. Those who mind do not matter, and those who matter don't mind. There are millions of insecure, entitled, disempowered women. They walk in their insecurity and in their fear of losing something, which was never there.

I See Myself

*If an idiot were to tell you the same story every day for a year,
you would end by believing it.*

—Horace Mann

I AM THE AUTHOR OF my own story, and yet I possess a capacity to give myself a supporting role. My husband, my parents, my children, and grandchildren are also authors, and I am also in their cast.

As for getting my story "right"—stories are not just the ones people tell us, but also the ones we tell ourselves. I knew I was smart, funny, and worthy of acceptance, but I still did not accept it as true. Defensively, I confined myself behind an unscalable wall. I never gave myself a chance to be honest with myself, or with others. And so, the consequences renewed each time I erred. Much of life does not turn out the way you plan.

God does not obey the rules; God makes the rules. The Hebrews were written to prosper more in the gospel than anyone, while the unlikely whoremongers and thieves fed from the root. In the Book of Revelation, Jesus commended the church at Ephesus for its many good works but was grieved because they had not kept their love for Him alive.

He said, "I know your works, your labor, your patience, and that you cannot bear those who are evil… Nevertheless, I have this against you, that you have left your first love" (Revelations 2:2-4). Deeds are not as important as a relationship with Jesus. He reminds His followers to stay close to Him and obey His commands or else they will not bear much fruit for Him. For without Him, they can do nothing.

In my youth, I resisted change. All I really wanted was a sense of belonging, without being compelled to make any changes. No matter what encouraging words others said about me, even my mother as growing up. I rejected them. She did the best she could with what she learned from her own upbringing. In fact, I believe my mom was one of best mothers in the world. In my profound sense of inadequacy, I never pursued the dreams she suggested, like becoming a model.

Barbizon, a modeling agency based in New York with an office in West Hartford I attend at eleven years old. I did not find it amusing enough for me at eleven. I did not like wearing make-up at the age eleven. I saw myself as Jon Benet Ramsey the little beauty queen who wore makeup. I thought this is a little too much for me. I'm older looking at photo shoots perhaps maybe considering pursing modeling, most photographers wanted nude sexy photos something I did not feel comfortable doing. I was flat chest a skinny girl not seeing how men looked at me as sexy at this time in my life. I thought this is something that I will no longer pursue. It amaze me how people got ahead for sex. However, the photographers would ask me to pose in suggestive ways. They wanted a *sexy* look, a *sexy* stance. None of it resonated with me.

How could people imagine or say remarkable things about me, and somehow, I knew it was not going to happen? I knew I would sabotage things for myself. My inability to love myself openly and honestly developed from a profoundly traumatic childhood experience.

Raped

Not everything that can be counted counts and not everything that counts can be counted.

—Albert Einstein

AN ADULT SEXUALLY ABUSED ME when I was about fourteen. I remember, it was the summer of my soon-to-be the first year in high school. I was right on target in age and in grade in school.

At the time, and for long after, I disassociated the assault. Any feelings about it seemed unfocused and disconnected from myself. Despite this, the attack held me captive. Only with kids my own age, who experienced the same or comparable situation, did I feel comfortable. As a result, I spent many years attempting to change my face to conform to whatever crowd was safest. I never trusted my feelings because I believed just being me was never enough. I did not earn the acceptance I deserved. I became so tired of living my life beneath my right. I am so tired of the devil turning a mirror on a distorted, uglier semblance of myself.

It was summertime, and school was out. Streetlights fluoresced. Young adults tore through the streets in cars, music blaring through open windows. And then there was me. Those days, I watched the proverbial clock for my fourteenth birthday, which wasn't coming fast enough. Yet it came. My best friend Cynt and I would walk to Divi-Divi, a local restaurant, which sold hamburgers, milkshakes, candy, and the long hotdogs on a toasted bun. Cynt always went for the cheeseburgers. I, on the other hand, did not get anything from them other than their long chili hotdogs. It was the walk we both enjoyed. We lived in the same apartment building upstairs from one another, and Divi-Divi was about fifteen minutes away walking slow in a hot humid evening.

One night, inside the restaurant while waiting for a cheeseburger and hotdog, we noticed a strange man. He sat out in his canary yellow El Dorado Cadillac. Probably late twenties, he had a chiseled face with a pug-like flat nose. His curly hair hung longer than any female I knew. Not attractive at all. I liked the car, though. Cynt and I glanced at one another as if through telepathy: *omg he is sho' 'nuf ugly.*

He came inside as if he forgot something, but I'm sure it was really to check out the young little girls who just arrived at the restaurant. I had a herringbone necklace I received from my mother when I graduated eighth grade into high school my first year of high school—a gift along with a new stereo system mother purchased from the mall for seven hundred dollars. My mother let me choose whichever necklace I wanted. And I wanted that one. Just as we thought about leaving, he started a conversation with us. He complimented my necklace. He asked if I liked jewelry, which caught me off guard.

"Yes," I replied.

"You have a phone number?" he continued forthrightly. "I've got some jewelry. I'll give you a call, and you can check out what I've got." A pause. "You'll like it," he added.

I did something I had no business doing. I gave this stranger my home phone number.

After Cynt and I got our order and were walking home, Cynt teased me. With a smirk, she said he liked me.

"Oh, no, he don't," I rebuffed her. "He said he had some jewelry he wanted me to see in case I wanted to buy."

Who offers jewelry to a child? Well, that grown-ass man did.

Cynt and I laughed all the way home as we wondered aloud why that lowlife asked for my phone number.

Cynt kept saying, "He coming for you, Wanda."

I laughed. "No, he is *not*."

We eventually ate our food in my home and ended the night.

The next morning, Cynt called me to ask if I wanted to walk to the store with her. Of course, I would—we did everything together. We would go to the store at least three or four times a day, especially in the summer. We always had money we got from allowances or winning Pokeno with her family.

Cynt, ever bounding with energy, was at my door before I could get myself together. Finally, I said, "Come on, I'm ready."

Just as we began to walk out, our house phone rang. I paused for a moment to decide if I should answer it or not, but I thought it might be my mother or grandmother calling, so I had better answer it. When I did, I heard a voice I didn't know. He asked to speak to Wanda.

"This is Wanda," I replied, my brow furrowed. "Who is this?"

"Vaugn," came the self-assured answer. "The man you met at Divi-Divi on Barbour Street. I have the jewelry I want to show you. Can you meet me at the same place I seen you at last night?"

"I'm on my way to the store with my friend."

"Which store are you going to? I would like to show you the jewelry."

I told him we were on our way to a place on Barbour Street called Leslie's.

"Okay," he said. "I know where it is, and I'm going to meet you there to show you the jewelry. I have to see if you like it."

When we arrived at the store, I noticed the same loud canary yellow Cadillac parked on the corner.

Standing on the sidewalk, Cynt teased me again. "He wants you."

I paid Cynt no mind.

Then, she said she would wait for me inside. I said I was just going to look at his jewelry and then I'd join her inside.

As I approached the passenger side of his car, he looked at me with that same angular face. Eying me, he asked me to get in so he could show me.

Immediately after I got in the car, he hit a button, which raised the passenger window, and pushed the door lock.

In a moment, his tone went cold. "You just got in the car of a pimp. Sit back, bitch."

Reeling, I didn't know what to think or do. I was terrified.

He careened down streets as if he were getting away from the scene of a crime. I could do nothing. Nothing, except watch out the window for any information I could use. I wanted to remember the street names. Somehow, I had to get away from this monster.

This lowlife, mediocre rapist saw the innocence of a young girl who he thought he could groom and make a lifelong whore out of. I was not cut from that cloth, and he would soon find out. This was his game of catching someone to work the streets for him. He wanted to solicit me to prostitute as a kid. I did not look like a whore and was very innocent. I had not given my virginity to anyone. He thought he was slick, zigzagging in and out of streets to distract me from where he was bringing me. I memorized every turn. The names of the streets were all I needed to know. He took me to a house he parked his car as if hiding it.

Drawing the key from the ignition, he said, "Get out."

I was terrified. Looking at him in a trance, I told myself, *I am about to get raped by this man.* We entered the house. He called over a Doberman, a large black dog with tall, pointed ears and militant obedience.

One by one, he took off his clothes and then got into the bed. I stood there, still in the shirt and pants I wore when I got into his car, telling myself, *this monster is not doing what he is doing.* But I was afraid of the big dog, and so, I slowly began removing my clothes. At the same time, I was thinking, *Am I really doing this? I need some help. This monster is about to rape me.*

Now butt-ass naked, he looked me up and down. I had no breasts, no curves, and besides that, I was little and frail. Who would want to do anything sexual with a kid? His glinting eyes seemed poised—for what, I did not understand.

He told me to get in the bed, and as I approached the covers, he positioned himself while lying on his back. Unabashedly, he asked me to suck his dick. *Oh my God. I have never done this.*

I sat there frozen, not believing he was asking me for this. I did not even know how to do it.

He asked, "You ever do this before?"

I told him no.

Suddenly, his hands reached for my belly. I could see the top of his head as he licked me. It was horrible. I could not fathom any of it. The sickening thought came: *this creep is raping me, and no one is here to help me.*

When he the idiot was done, I turned my back to him in disgust. It lasted a total of three minutes, but it felt like an eternity.

Once he raped me, he got up unceremoniously and went into the bathroom to wash himself with a towel. Then, he brought me a wet rag. As I washed myself, I saw there was blood. I felt sore and like crap.

Each time he looked at me, I saw in his haunted eyes—he knew he had gotten himself into serious trouble. He could not have made me feel any better, but oh, how he tried. He even tried to talk to me as if we were lovers. This guy, who had only just met me at the neighborhood restaurant, clothed in a friendly façade, and manipulated me into giving him my home phone number. This creature was a pedophile and a rapist. I imagined how many other women he played this game on to try to get to prostitute for him. Pathetic. This loser no doubt had terrible DNA, which followed him for life. If this was the only way for him to catch a woman, then catching women was not the game for him. This behavior comes from not having your very own identity. He was an unattractive man with big, thick, bouncy curls, like a woman whose hair rollers had just been freshly removed at the hair salon. We as society see men such as these as child molesters someone who go out their way to have sex with kids. If there be anyone you may know who has dated or looked upon a child while they were ever over twenty years old pushing thirty are a rapist no excuse and while you are reading my book and if this is you than you are a rapist, period. We need to keep in mind these same men have children- history repeats itself. This is when they should try to do everything in their power to break this unruly generational curse that easily beset us today. I do not care whomever you are to look upon a child with lust is a sin and disgusting, you have a problem, you need healing and deliverance for your soul. We as people need to be remindful not to leave our kids or grandkids in the presences of people especially if you know there are concerns or any suspicion of anyone who are likely to commit this crime and it runs in their family. Some of us are so quickly to get a sitter for our kids or while someone else kids are in your custody to watch other people kids not caring who they are, unacceptable. We have the family members who grown children has done things such as molestation or sexual things to their children's kids and beg you not to get the authorities or department of family services involved. These are people who do not wish to see anything bad happen to their family members, quick to call law enforcement or tell on anyone. How sick are they? This same thing happens when outside relatives allowed this very same thing to happen to their young kids and tried to cover it up because it was their immediate family and their child. I have seen this in my family as a child to an adult. And this is sick stuff. Those who cover up for these sick people are sicker.

I dressed from that disgusting episode of being forced to do something I did not want to do. He then drove me downtown to a wig store, where the man who worked inside styled the wigs. This man, who flamboyantly greeted my rapist, may have known him personally. I could not believe the stylist picked a long wig to place on me. I thought I would die once I looked in the mirror. The more I beheld my reflection, the more my anger rose in me. We were the only folks in the store. My rapist knew how frightened he had me even before he drove me downtown in broad daylight. Simultaneously, I did not want anyone to notice me, in a wig, with this monster as we crossed the street to get in his big, bright-yellow Batmobile Cadillac.

To him, the car screamed luxury, and of course, he needed to have someone "fine" in it—again, I was just fourteen—but to me, the car was as ugly as him. While downtown, he reached for my hand to hold it as if he knew I would run.

My heart drumming, I searched the perimeter for a police officer in the area. My window for rescue waned with each step toward his car. One passed I caught the flash of a blue uniform, cuffs reflecting sunlight. But the officer was too far away.

I did not want to be beaten by this man in the street. Now, I believe he would not have made any attempt such as but to only scare the living day lights out of me, him hitting anyone in the streets of a downtown would have drawn considerable amount of attention, something he did not want. What a sucker walking around downtown with someone kid holding her hand proud you kidnapped her sic. I was so afraid, though I could not risk it. However, I wanted to scream for help, seeing myself do it but not doing it. He was someone who has did this before repeatedly to young kids. He felt the need he snatch me up, this beautiful kid, he would have me for a lifetime. The devil was really filling his head with all sorts of lies.

The innocent little girl in me was so afraid. My parents did not raise us in violence. I was not someone who were beat or in fights. I know without any shadow of doubt, if my father had not been in prison, I would be protected by this predator, and this would not have happened to me. I would never have given him our home phone number – an action I considered only adults do. Rather he had jewelry he wanted to sell me or not.

This jerk could clearly see I was a child. All while we were in his car, he continually said we were going to New York. His upbeat tone suggested I had at some point, enthusiastically agree to his plan. New York was just two hours away. I just wanted to be found and back home with my family. I did not have any money other than the few small bills I had to go to the corner store with Cynt to buy snacks that morning. Our usual was Stateline chips a bottle of coke and a twinkie.

This lowlife was under the impression I could be trained to prostitute myself for him. I can look back at this situation and see how other young female girls who may have run away from their homes, got themselves in trouble decided to find themselves doing such a thing called prostitution for someone because they may have needed to live somewhere or eat. This was not my case, nor it was something I ever thought about for anyone. He did not realize the female he thought he would be using to train me to prostitute would be the one who did not wish to have her, or her pimp's name involved in any crime as kidnap and sexual assault because they were living life on life terms living in a Penthouse on Lexington Ave in NY city. The couple had arrived in this life and Vaughn was trying to get there, at his age not having his very own apartment. I have never seen anyone live this lifestyle from prostitution ever only in the movies. He did not know the young lady would soon bring me to the port authority, so I could inform the authorities I'm missing and needs to be returned home. Who would run off with a kid and take her out of state to dress her up to solicit? A sic individual who has unexamined childhood issues.

The inspiration you seek is already within you. Be silent and listen.

—Rumi

Our dignity is not in what we do, but what we understand.

—George Santayana

I was not alone. The prostitute saw to it she taken me to the port authority, where she informed the authorities, I was a missing child. Then, like a gust of wind, she left. Surely, she wanted no further involvement in my abduction. I watched as the cashier printed me a ticket while she dialed the police.

The New York Police Department office must have telephoned the Hartford police department, who contacted my mother. Officers put me on a Greyhound bus.

"Stay here," they directed me, "until you get to Hartford. An officer in a cruiser will meet you there." I did as told by the officer.

In Hartford, yet another officer asked my name, date of birth, and my mother's phone number. He wanted to know what happened.

I had waited for this moment—with the memory still raw—I told him everything.

When I was through, he said I would go with him to the hospital, where my mother would meet me. Though excited to return, I was not excited to tell my mother about the last two days. Yet, I knew I had to.

The moment I saw my mother, it was as if she had just given birth to me all over again. We were both overjoyed to be together once more. As I knew she would, my mom had reported me missing to the local police department.

One of the officers showed me a photo.

He asked, "Is this him?" I told him yes.

Next, after the reunion and the police, I was ushered into an ER examination room. All evidence collected would build a case against the creep. The nurse collected semen he ejaculated in me. The staff also wanted to make certain he did not leave me with any STIs. Prior to being discharged, the nurse asked my mother if she wished me to have counseling, but my mom said no. She wanted to get me home and forget about all of this. However, she was not so eager to unshackle this creep from what he'd done to her little girl. She wanted him to pay.

After I told her all he did to me, I promised her I would never go anywhere else or get into anyone's car again. There are other men in this line of business who would most definitely kidnap young girls, imprison them as slaves, usurp their power, and rape them. I have always thought men like him must use women to get what they need because no real man mistreats a lady.

A person must be sick to do something like what he did to me.

Mother should have had me talk to a therapist. Grateful as I was to be home with my family, it was heartache to share my terrible story with them. I did not know I needed a professional to work with me. Sometime not long ago after, mom asked me whether I wish to go to counseling? I said no. I said I was great, truly both she and I had issues we were unable to identify or intimate to one another. We should have sought counseling.

My mother believed she had the courage and the love in God to heal me. She turned the aftermath over to God in prayer and trusted Him to punish that man. Through this experience and others, I realized my family habitually keeps sensitive secrets so closely that unless you knew about something as it was happening, you would never know at all. Only because of a specific circumstance did I learn, for example, my mom's sister had a baby by a white man at the age of fourteen. It was said she was raped but in reality, her brother who was my favorite uncle told the story she had sex with a married man as being a babysitter for the couple. My aunt later married and gave birth to more children, but her first child always felt like an outcast.

I would sometimes hear Mom on the phone with her mom, my grand-mother, saying, "God is going to get the man who raped her." I waited for that day to come.

And then, it did.

We heard Vaugn preached from a church pulpit, dressed like a pimp with a super-sized, larger-than-life hat brim, hair tumbling with curls, his legs crossed like the last crippled homo. Soon after, there was talk he no longer attended services. He had a nervous breakdown and went into an asylum or rehab. Mental health issues tangled him up inside, and at once, it all came crashing down.

Today, he rides a bicycle. His appearance unkempt, he reminds me of a homeless man chasing joy and escaping from life. To avoid coping with trauma is to invite cognitive disease and emotional imbalance. Many of us emerge from our trauma confused, unaware of how or unable to reckon with it. There comes a point when we must trust someone with our pain. No, it is never easy! It was challenging to acknowledge my faults to myself, let alone admit them to someone else. Costly mistakes linger in my past, which is a fact I have had to accept.

One day, it was nearly time for school when our phone rang. The Hartford police informed mom and I they had this creature in custody. They wanted to know when they could come by.

The two officers who came to our home said, "Vaughn will be going to court soon, and I will need you to be there."

They told me where to report when I arrived and told Mom and me where to go to meet the state's attorney. Based on my description, they noticed the bright-yellow Cadillac with three white women—one driving, one on the passenger side, and one in the back—with Vaughn.

When they pulled his vehicle over, lights flashing, they knew Vaughn was afraid. He knew he'd be picked up for what he had done to me; it was why he ushered only white women into the car. White women are seen by some as a symbol of status. Whether hungry to feel like a king, or hiding in the backseat, he must have known a warrant was out for his arrest.

He leaned on a cane as he stepped out of the car. This detail, which spoke to his lifestyle, is one burned into my memory. The white women did not bother to bail him out, so he remained in custody until he was sentenced.

The case appeared in the *Hartford Courant*, although, since I was underage, it omitted my name. With school back in session, I told people what happened to me. I absolutely included his name.

I never expected to hear from people who knew him—let alone defended him.

Despite living in the same area as Vaugn, I hadn't known him prior to the Divi-Divi encounter. As he was older than either my siblings or me, we had zero connection.

The world, however, is smaller than I would have liked. Vaugn's ugly sister Deb heard who I was from someone—I suspect Cynt's sister. They all went to the same high school. Deb appeared identical to Vaugn in many ways. She possessed the same angular face and pug-like nose, and besides those features, her rotund body, short hair, and nasty demeanor rendered her incredibly unattractive. I have learned unattractive women without redeeming qualities always act out or differentiate themselves for validation. In Deb's case, her physical ugliness angered her.

She was a known bully. My youthful age seemed not to give her pause. Repeatedly, she sent me threats—not in person, but through a neighbor in the same high school. I paid them no mind. I didn't care who she was, although I took note of her character. She thought if she could force me not to attend court, her brother would be free of any charges. One day, I received a message she would beat me up.

Though unfazed, I did not like hearing garbage from a sex offender's sister. He was a rapist. A child rapist. He the rapist had been caught! His entire family must have suffered from serious mental issues to not only violate young girls, but to threaten them into silence.

In the witness box, I described the creature who raped me. Black, flat face, long, curly hair extending to his shoulders, and ugly. I will never forget what he looked like.

The matter wrapped up very quickly in court. I easily identified him in a lineup. I was determined the lowlife would not go free. If released, he would rape again. He would use the same insane tactics to catch little girls and force them to work. He's been released since then, and I'm certain he has done it again—probably over and over again.

After he was found guilty, he accepted the first offer because it would carry less time in jail. Typically, accepting an offer like it would cut a sentence by as much as ninety percent, but the violent nature of the crime barred him from the full benefit. My father was also in prison, but the court did not send Vaughn to the same one. They kept him at the local jail with a three-year sentence.

I have learned to recognize people for who they really are, including their faults—a practice called the Discernment of Spirits. It is a pivotal gift from God. When you recognize it, you receive more gifts from God. I discern when there is a pedophile, rapist, addict, an absorber, or a manipulator around. These spirits take from others. Because I recognize them, malicious spirits no longer dwell in my life, or our children or grandchildren's lives. I live to protect my family, so creatures cannot do what they did to me.

Since early childhood, I had visions and dreams of who I was and what type of man I wanted to be involved with. I wanted someone with the same values, morals, and principals as I. I learned, however, one might hold dearly to his own values, which differ from mine.

Cynt had a cousin named Moochie. Moochie thought he was a player, both in and out of the boxing ring. We were kids then; he was ten, and I was nine. We would talk on the phone just before bed or after playing Pokeno at Cynt's house with her mother, aunt, and cousin. We played for hours and left with the money we won. It was exciting. Cynt and me always split our kitty—our winnings—at the end of the night. We would win as much as eighty dollars.

As we grew up, my infatuation also grew. We both lived in the housing project in Bellevue Square, although I did not know him when my family lived there. I met Cynt only after my parents moved to a better place. She and I would watch him box. We would go out for the weekend to Jimmy's Seafood Restaurant, and sometimes we would stop at a club in New Haven just to dance.

I knew Moochie was in the limelight. He loved being with different women. A confirmed bachelor, he lived alone and made all his decisions. All the women he spent time with thought they would be his wife, but it never happened. Moochie was also cheap. I remember one year; he gave out photos of himself as gifts. Yes the photos came with cheap thin frames, I was struck by the lackluster present. Still, we were only friends, so I accepted it.

His other women were older than me and thought he would marry them because two had a baby by him. Although I never looked at him as anything other than a friend, I knew, even given a distinct perspective, he would not marry me. He was too much of a whore; I could never trust him. I let go moved on. He still wanted to be friends still and we are today no bad blood cool. So, we were friends without attachments. I allowed him to be my friend because we had no ill feelings, no arguments, and no fights. We understood one another. I had my own idea of what I wanted in the man I longed for. When his girlfriend's heard about me, he told them I was his friend, and they had no other choice but to accept it. They wanted what we had.

As time passed, we spoke in passing. I let him know I was getting married. After three years dating my fiancé, I felt the need to finally get married. In fact, my fiancé asked me to marry him only three months into dating, and I had accepted. Affectionate and principled, my fiancé was the only one for me; I knew this for sure. Thirteen years my senior, he reminded me of the father figure I never had. We always held hands whenever we were out. We both enjoyed it. He came from good stock with great parents, and we agreed on morals and values. Plus, he knew how to treat me with all I ever deserved. This man bought me custom jewelry made at a high-end jeweler. This had me excited and feeling worthy of his love. I mean, come on! A two-carat diamond ring, one-carat diamond earrings, two-carat single diamond bracelets, and David Yurman earrings and bracelets… I was nineteen years old going on twenty, and I was finally getting everything I wanted.

A Life of Crime

They always say time changes things, but you actually have to change them yourself.

—Andy Warhol

We inhabit ourselves without valuing ourselves, unable to see that here, now, this very moment is sacred; but once it's gone—its value is incontestable.

—Joyce Carol Oates

MY EXPERIENCES INFORM MY REALITY. My story has nothing to do with anyone except me. Everyone has a different perception of the same life experiences. As a result, different people tell different stories about the same occurrence. My truth is, I diligently searched for an excuse to be lazy. I ignored the voice in my spirit.

This is my story about how personal defects can lead one to the edge of one's personal power. By loving and accepting myself, I can jump headfirst into greatness.

Even ostensibly insignificant events can be defining moments. I say, do the right thing; even if it is difficult, the easy way out is only temporary. What we do in our defining moments will make or break us. When we let our feelings rule us, we never make good choices. Do not satisfy a short-term appetite at the expense of a long-term blessing. Not only do we miss God's best opportunities when we make such choices, we also negatively influence our children.

In challenging circumstances, people may hurt us. Pain can motivate us to indulge in pettiness. Stay peaceful, for God awaits us on His throne. I was trapped, stuck between my past and future, unsure which path to choose. I had it so good for so long, hustling became second nature to me. I manufactured schemes, committed credit card, wire, and check fraud, and manipulated people. When I was much younger, I told people: *you are going to pay me half your proceed whomever worked for me and they did. You will pay me directly—no interception at all. With my skills, I made it happen.* All I knew was organized crime.

I did unacceptable things because, from sixteen through eighteen years old, no one properly supervised me. My mother worked third shift. I mostly stayed inside and off the streets, where many women worked as "street chicks." I was never the type to run away from home; it was never in my psyche.

What I *would* do was look at fashion magazines. I envied the glamour the status of it all. I decided what I needed was to seize a wealthy lifestyle. I ordered things from the stores with credit cards I took from doctors who never knew their information was stolen. I traveled out of state and committed the same crimes. Sometimes, I used others' credit cards and checks to go shopping. Some of you may wonder how I got these cards. I took them while teachers were at recess or not in their classrooms. Staff at private hospitals and companies left them at their stations or desks. I was never afraid. I got a kick out of the way I scored. I even read in the newspaper about crimes I committed. The thrill kept me spiritually stuck. Meanwhile, detectives investigated, but had no leads.

Crime became fascinating to me. A rush swept over me, followed by a compulsion to do more and get more. I quit well-paying jobs to focus on shopping and scheming. Only later did it become something I no longer wanted to do.

I hired a private plan to wait for me while I rode a taxi to a bank. I paid for a block of hours, which was exorbitantly expensive. I was not worried. I was about to come into some money, I knew it. This was my hustle.

While in the bank, the teller wanted to verify my transaction. He reached out to the doctor whose information I'd taken. Fortunately—for me—the teller happened to call when the doctor was in surgery, so he left a message with the secretary. The teller informed the branch manager the doctor was occupied; the manager, intoxicated, called the surgeon to verify the check. I immediately left the bank. From a payphone, aware the number I was using was blocked from callers id. I called the doctor's office to tell them we called his office, but there was an error. I was extraordinarily lucky the doctor was still in surgery. He never received the call from the bank manager. By the time the doctor received the message, I told them the bank would close, and they did not need to call back.

The secretary was fine with it. I then called the bank, pretended I was the doctor's secretary, and authorized payment of the check.

"I'm coming in soon," I said. "Have the manager talk to me. I'll be in a chair in the lobby." I was ecstatic about how it all worked out. Upon entering the bank, I sat in a chair as if I had been there all along and waited. This company was large, and its operating hours stretched long into the evening.

The branch manager, an African American woman, noticed me and approached. I'd already noted her intoxication. She said, since the office called to speak with the bank, they would honor my funds. I was on point to call from the payphone. Tickled as if driving in high gear, I nodded my approval.

Everything fell into place exactly as I planned. I had asked for the manager by name specifically so I could manipulate her each step in the process. She seemed like she worked best while drinking on the job.

Without delay, I wrote a check for seven thousand dollars, and I received every penny. I left, got in my taxi, and climbed aboard my chartered flight. We stayed at a four-star hotel in the Maryland area, and I felt the urge to find some card numbers to play with. I thought it would be a good time I could make some large purchases from my hotel room. I contacted the desk to get a card number by offering a room number or guessing a popular name. Whomever answer your call not inattentively listening, busy hotel immediately is going to go to the room or last name immediately and give you their info when they hear authorization wasn't approved. There have been times in a huge hotel where customer wish not to go to desk and you call to say the authorization failed do you have your card in your possession? And the card number is? Immediately you're given their info. They're believing being they just checked in it's believable. I'm sure things are more extreme stringent even out of country now a days. In fact, on my first try the representative gave me the card number than said" you mean for secret service agent Mr. John Doe. Immediately I was afraid. I told her no Frank Weber any o' name just to let her know it was a mistake not worrying if she contacted him prior. I did not expect to get a credit card number of a secret service agent ever. I looked at the number as I written it tore it in pieces and flushed it down the toilet and taken a whiff of fresh air. I thought I had been given the card of a secret service agent. Discarding the number, I tried again. If you knew the cardholder's name and said your transaction was not approved in error, the representative could provide the card number. I checked out of the luxurious paid room.

I was far from the only one to defraud others. I read stories like this for instance in the newspaper. I read about an interracial couple who received a credit card they never used by the time they discovered their bill their high credit line was already used. All I knew their bill was becoming due for payment and it being a American Express Card. It had no limit at this time. The only way the couple knew anything about their card was receiving a bill in the mail. They reported their card stolen. However, the authorities believed the couple used their card being the man was black. How I learned of this information the police questioned me and I did not know anything just listened to them.

Writing a fraudulent doctor's check was not the first time I forged a signature, nor was it the only time I hired a private plane. I used a corporate account to hire the plane. When I arrived undercover officials met me. As soon as I signed the invoice for the flight, they pulled out their badges and placed me under arrest. I had a feeling it was not a smart move, but I did it anyway. I appeared in court and had to pay the cost of the flight, even though I never used it.

I would creep into small businesses operated in wealthy towns. Staff would take out the deposit bags and leave them unattended in their store or business. One day, I entered one such store and had someone distract the owner. It was not necessary, though. Entirely preoccupied, she never even knew I was inside.

In no time, I was in my car and gone. The two deposit bags contained estate jewelry valued at one hundred thousand dollars. There was also cash in the amount of least ten to twenty thousand dollars.

Yet foolish and young I went back to the same town to go to the grocery store alone. The owner of the shop I removed two money bags loaded the day prior seen me in a local grocery store in this wealthy town wearing her jewelry too unnoticeable. The very next day, I was at home when the doorbell rang. I answered it without asking who it was. When I opened the door, I discovered it was a local secret service agent.

The agent asked about the vehicle seen the day I shopped at the grocery store. The woman was only able to get the license plate of the vehicle, which was a rental in my mother's name. I had rented a car with my mom's paper driver's license; at that time, there was no photo on the license.

I immediately told the agent I was driving the car, and my mother had nothing to do with anything. He already knew this. He then left, completed his report, and filed a warrant for my arrest. I already had at least three to four arrests at this point, which were all larceny, including one case in Superior Court, then this was added. I posted bond same day I met with my attorney Mack Buckley who represented me on all my cases for many years. He remains one of the greatest defense attorneys around. Avvo, a rating site for attorneys, rated Mack as a Super Star 10, the highest possible score. He had his own insight of people. He knew exactly how to execute his strategy when it came to winning. A wordsmith, he curated his words to fit any situation, just as would any highly educated prosecutor who values high conviction rates in their own practices.

There are things one does which enslaves them to habits and patterns. Habits and patterns become addictions. I developed an addiction to finer things. I always needed money. I was in such denial about being an addict. And when I say addict, I mean my soul was also affected. These are the traits I saw in my dad—traits I was attracted to at an early age. I would sabotage goals I set up for myself in order to satisfy my cravings. My cravings were all material. Although I'm not proud of this fact, it's a part of me.

Today, I reflect on my past with respect to contemporary crime. Our forty-fifth president, Donald J. Trump, behaved similarly to how I once did. The only difference is that he was president. His crimes reached higher than mine ever did. He is a persistent career repeated offender who the government allowed to get away with his crimes along with his former staff: William Barr, Rudy Giuliani, Mick Mulvaney, Mike Pompeo, John Bolton, Vice President Mike Pence, Defense Attorney Mark Esper, and those whom officials do not name. These men have done wrong harmed more people taken the lives of millions of people in the pandemic of Covid-19 knowing withholding this information. Donald Trump must be accountable for his actions, yet escape prison time; meanwhile, the judicial system sentences petty criminals to time not proportional to what they have done. We see how the system work for some and how it works for others—like me who's black. I shared crimes I have seen, and there are many more I refuse to talk about. The system does not play fair toward our own. It makes one say *fuck*!

Sister's Rage

People pay for what they do, and still more for what they have allowed themselves to become. And they pay for it very simply; by the lives they lead.

—James Baldwin

A man's enemies will be the members of his own household.

—Matthew 10:36

MY OLDER SISTER KNUCKIE WAS a blue-eyed, Afro-American, high-yellow child, who won the national baby contest in 1954. She was my parents' first—a daddy's girl.

They almost lost her when she was five. She was hit by a club owner's car and pronounced dead on the scene. Mother prayed for God to let her baby live, and He did. I had not yet been born. My dad's love grew for his daughter during the tragedy. The doctor told my mother if Knuckie live, she will have mental health issues for the rest of her life. My parents did not care; they only wanted their child alive.

Her mental health issues, however, posed a problem for me. As I grew up, she told her male friends she was my mother. Most of them flirted with me or complimented my appearance. She criticized what I wore and how I looked. I did not understand why until mother told me, at twenty years old, my sister envied me. The revelation hurt so badly. She was my only sister—the oldest of us all. Mother said she did not know why Knuckie was so jealous of me. One day, I confronted Knuckie about it. She told me Mom always favored me; Mom always showed off my photos to houseguests, including the insurance agent, the service guy, relatives—everyone.

I began to see she did not like herself. Just before losing our mother, we discovered my sister had changed all my mother's beneficiaries on her life insurance policies. Knuckie had cancelled any with my name or my children listed. I deposited a check my mother requested from her insurance company. I signed her name to the check for deposit, which Mom gave me permission to do. I had cared for Mom six days a week, and I would return home just to rest. Meanwhile, Knuckie gambled with the money she stole from Mother at every casino she could find. Because of my sister, I was arrested four months after we lowered Mother into her grave. Knuckie was dangerously angry about her illnesses and the loss of her only child. Although I sympathized, I knew this was not how one heals from mental and physical health struggles, which will slowly kill her as well.

The memories of what Knuckie did are still painful. I lived in and survived prison. As soon as I posted bail, another warrant surfaced five weeks later. The warrant left me with no funds to pay my rent, car loan, car insurance, personal loans, or credit cards. I have learned how my sister feels about me is not my fault. I sat in prison on trumped-up charges because of my sister's jealousy. My conviction as a felon made these arrests even more punishing.

To this day, I don't understand why she felt so inadequate. Whenever I'm not in her presence, she always speaks badly about me. Even if we had just ate and had fun at a restaurant together, it just never seemed to stop with her. I did not feel the need to be in her presence or experience her behavior forever. Sometimes, we would get along—we'd talk, and I'd share with her about things I have done. We would laugh about it, and I chalked her past mistakes up to youth and smoked marijuana at home.

As a teenager and young adult, Knuckie would lie about my personal business to my mother. I decided I could not, even in good times, share secrets with her. After a while, she noticed my reservation. She suspected I had more funny stuff to say. I refused, however, to share anything more at my expense.

When she saw me, she always noisily complemented and inquired about my jewelry, clothing, hairstyles, cars, home business, and furniture. Whatever it was she noticed, she wanted it for herself. She reminded me of women on the street who did or did not know me who were just haters. But she was my sister.

When I was arrested after burying our mom I turned myself into authorities. I took a plea. It tore me away from my children, which pained me profoundly. Knuckie was hurting from the loss of her only child, yet this was no excuse to marionette in other people's lives. She did not know how to heal independently.

I had visions of killing her. While I cried in a prison cell, I told God how I hated her. My mind, I told Him, led me to her doorstep; graphically vivid, it showed me shooting her and waiting for the police to arrive. It played repeatedly inside my head. But the Holy Spirit intervened. The Spirit reminded me of my talents, skills, abilities, and gifts. It said I needed to use them. *Knuckie*, it told me, *would love to see you in prison for the rest of your life because she did not have a life of her own.*

I praised God and promised Him I'd do His will. I'd put away foolish thoughts. I was frightened, but not of lifelong incarceration. I thought about my grandchildren—how much I would miss them and how much I needed to be in their lives. I reflected on my actions, which imprisoned me in the past and recognized them anew as selfish.

I discovered what Knuckie resents about me are our differences. And being different, she wanted to be like me in one way or another. Unlike her, I am a hustler. I have always been independent and self-sufficient, something our mom instilled in me more than any of her other children. Our parents saw varying skills and personalities in each of us. As a child, I would always share ideas about what I would like to become and do for myself. When we were much younger, Knuckie perceived my relationship with Mother as particularly close. I was the baby of four children, until our mother married again when I was thirteen years old Mother had another baby being I was her last from my father. Mother had remarried to my stepdad, and they shared a son together. Moe we all had to care for him as they both worked. Our siblings favored me. I was always there for everyone in our household. I have always been a giver not a taker and never a hater. We loved each other immensely.

As time passed it was always the same issue with Knuckie, the only conclusion I can fathom was she was mad she was not able to do what I do. She felt incompetent. What she did not know is there are strategies and skills to what one does, which becomes a career, whether morally good or bad.

This chick so angry she went out her way to tell authorities one of my sons killed her son, which we knew was not true. She resented the fact I got what I wanted from God; six beautiful children. I always wanted babies. I envisioned marriage, the perfect home with a picket fence, horses, and a dog. I am naturally a nurturer, while my sister is not. When I was a teenager, Mother asked me to help care for my baby brother. Mother said Knuckie did not have a mother's instinct and toddlers need this.

The older I became the worse our relationship became not good at all. I do not believe a lot of family members knew any of this until our mother's illness and passing. I have decided to not ever deal with her again. Yet she played her cards similar the same way toward me being grimy. This was nothing I care to do. I have learned not to be around her. She would call me and ask when I was coming over some sick stuff huh?

This is where I would say "you would like to have me around with the way you talk about me? Why?"

She would deflect with another lie. I just could not hold on to her chaos. Although Knuckie was our mom's power of attorney, Mother had to add another sibling because Knuckie was stealing from her twenty thousand at a time from her. When Mother revealed this to me, Knuckie being afraid now placing the blame on whomever she can my brother Moe. Both siblings were doing the same thing: they both pointed their fingers at the other as Mother's money continued to walk away twenty thousand at a time.

Knuckie stole forty thousand at least from Mother and got away with it. She blamed it on the cost of our mother's medication which mom requested. Although most of all mother's prescriptions were covered by her medical coverage. Yet Knuckie was a black card player at the casino, to be a black card player she had to spend three hundred thousand dollars at the casinos. She was caught out in her gambling addiction bad. Her entire wealth from her son's death benefits went to the casinos. This was her only way to medicate from the loss of her only child. What Knuckie really bought was casino points to get back what she already gave them out of the five-hundred thousand dollars she received from two insurance companies from the loss of her son.

Our parents knew we were all different. Whenever Dad, who was still married at the time, took Knuckie to visit his various girlfriends, she kept things quiet and did not tell a soul. It was another story anytime I went with him to visit another woman. I would tell my mother quickly. I was her baby, and I thought this was the right thing to do. I remember Mother being all right with it. As I grew older, mother told me stories about Dad and how, behind her stoicism, she was hurt. Their crumbling marriage bothered my father. He did not know what to do nor did he put any energy into something unaffected by his sincere efforts. If he did, it would have showed. I believed he did not understand how to do it. My dad knew on the inside of his mind what he and mom vows were to be. And hopefully one day they will do to death do we part. It happened. He knew he had a wife who is faithful and loved him. Mother spent all her time working and in church. Her life was church; I grew up in a small storefront Pentecostal church. I think my dad felt us drifting away.

As for Knuckie—I am her deliverer. She hates our differences. I now understand the story of Cain and Abel.

She believes I am better than she is. It bothers her immensely, regardless of my past, which is the only thing she uses against me—a terrible behavior that reminds me of the spiteful women I met in prison.

Today, I love my sister as I always have. My love for her has taken its toll, and I have had to regain my center by understanding she will always be the person she is. I would believe and think differently if she read books to learn more and acquaint herself with positive people who do positive work. Just being in the presence of anyone who does not lift themselves up is aversive to me. These types of people are insecure, uneducated, shallow, reluctant to change, and do not know what to do with themselves. I'll tell you—it's hard when you have done nothing positive all your life. Such people don't know where to start or how to begin.

Every man's memory is his private literature.

—Aldous Huxley

There are folks who sacrifice their blessings for hate, and it's sad. I try not to acquaint myself with people who do not love themselves, for the relationship invites demons to grab hold of one's mind and soul.

As I sat in prison for the last time (due to Knuckie's lies), my sister seized the opportunity to keep all of our mother's possessions. Mother had lots of high-scale antiques—furniture, dishes, fine art paintings, old medical and history books dated 1846–1920, and more. Mother wanted them to be handed to all of us siblings as was specifically stated in family meetings.

Knuckie did not want me to have anything. She went to a hearing in probate court and lied. She told a magistrate she sold Mother's antiques to pay bills, and she did not get enough money. It was a sob story. Every other week, she had yard sales to sell off Mother's estate. She did everything in her power to imitate my character. I had successful yard sales out in Mother's yard earned over five hundred dollars every time. While I conducted those sales for fun, Mother also loved to rid herself of things she did not need. The things Knuckie sold, on the other hand, were of immense value to our mother whereas it could have been left in the family as mother suggested. But when you are in need nothing more matters when one is in control and have a urgent need that needs to be met.

One day, while driving, I passed Knuckie. She was sitting out in the yard under a tree with all the furnishings out of Mother's garage strewn about the lawn. She was having a yard sale with my aunt Jo there helping her. I could not believe what I saw. She remembered how I had yard sales in mother's yard being terribly busy with customers. And she thought this was her chance to try to outdo me at a yard sale. How unrelated.

I remember having yard sales on Mother's front lawn on Saturdays and Sundays for years. Visitors purchased nonstop. We got rid of all the clutter, and we collected a decent amount of extra money. The utility of the sales doubled as a good chance to buy some of Mother's treasures from her dirt cheap. One day, Mom decided to give me her mother of pearl box, for which she paid about seven hundred dollars. Knuckie was furious.

Mother wanted us to love and be there for one another. She asked for this before going home to rest her soul and spirit. She passed after Kuckie had already cancelled Mother's life insurance policy she had through her employer for me and my brother Moe. A benefit mother paid for over forty years with a total value of one hundred and seventy thousand dollars. Mother worked at her job for forty-eight years. A policy that was merely paid for.

In another instance, Knuckie cosigned on an apartment for me. She insisted I just sign her name since she did not want to drive out of town to the management office. When probation called her to confirm all what I told them we were cool. They called her cell phone, and we were in the presence of one another. She had a plan, and I really did not know anything about it until I notice she resents me without any love or remorse. I could not phantom anything less. I not ever once believed my sister had it in her to do anyone this way never mind her sister. I no longer a homeowner felon two big strikes against me. I not ever once believed my sister had it in her to do anyone this way never mind my sister. This is an act of a sick, lonely, miserable misfit.

I spoke to my probation officer months later he remembered their conversation as well as had notes he taken concerning this matter. I only thought I would have to deal with this matter in court knowing Knuckie had gone out her way to harm me again to keep me away from mother's estate. I had no other choice but to be there for Mother and all that it required of me. Currently, I was looking into Mother's insurance policies for her. She had penny policies as well as big policies and Knuckie did not wish to for me to uncover all she had did to mother policies placing a code word on them something I have done handling mother affairs in things. The moment Knuckie realized I had been informed by representatives. I mentioned it in front of mother. She panicked. All of everything in her went into a different mode. She was saying terrible things about me to keep the focus off her to quickly have me behind bars. She knew I would have a big bond. All hell had broken out of all her trifling things she has been doing to keep mothers funds locked down for herself. Knuckie were doing all of this while mother was alive on her last stage. She filed a complaint with the management office and police department. Mother were terribly upset to hear the property manager called to say my sister is there in the office and I need to come down. A forty-minute drive at least. I screamed I was not going anywhere. I do not care what that bitch does. Mother yelled she is lying. I had to comfort mother and did not care to allow her to hear any of what was going on, yet she did. I hung up the phone. Mother said, "she does not understand why your sister do not like you or me"?

This is my reality. I'm not the only one who experience anything like this. I tell my story for others and myself. The antagonism with Knuckie never stopped. My insight sheds light on family issues. One's character for some people, persist indefinitely.

Nothing happened until after Mother passing, she was in the ground. I had been told by an officer who left his card in my door I have a warrant turn myself in. I had to post bond on a crime I was not guilty of. Soon after all the chaos I receive another call saying from my attorney saying the Chief States Attorneys office called to say I have another warrant. These folks were not playing fair at all believing all Knuckie was saying about me to get me sent to prison. No one ever considered if she may have some involvement herself. I could not believe the judicial system did not go as far as contacting probation nor did the lousy lawyer. I paid him two thousand dollars for the case. It was only about getting me behind bars again. I had strict probation they call it any arrest sends you back to prison as parole does.

I accepted a plea deal, meanwhile Knuckie was residing in her client's home as a live-in. Knuckie mistreated this client who was over 104 at the time. Knuckie talked about it as if it were nothing. I could not believe she spit in the client's face because the client spit in her face. She always paid me to watch her client while she traveled out of state to the casinos. While she was away gone longer than she anticipated the client patiently waiting for her arrival and when she did not show she called to tell her client she will be gone a little longer – day 4, her client called her agency to say she did not wish to have her back there to her house because she has left and have been paid and have someone else there caring for her. The client was assertive smart and coherent. She had family visiting her every other week and received phone calls every day speaking to them. This client did not have the coherent of anyone 104-years old-perhaps late seventies. Knuckie had taken from this client the big mistake was when I worked and abused her finances it all fell on me instead. The police department who typed the statement wrote what he wanted in the statement. A warrant filed against me. The officer wrote what he wanted to not to involve Knuckie to keep it her word against mine I'm last working for client. Everyone who would work for the client from lawn care to accountant was stealing from this client and no one questioned their actions. They wrote their own check. The bail that was set was for seven-hundred and fifty thousand dollars. My bond was higher than inmates who has murder charges. The defendant on the murder charges had gruesome murder charges. The victim was Black and pregnant. A Black man and white woman did this. The judicial system made it look like the white woman was sentenced to fifty-two years. She became an informant went against her boyfriend. The court gave the Black man her charges knew he would not see day light again. She lied and told a story she is going back to court to get a lesser sentence. She knew all the while she was promised she would get back in court for a sentence modification under a snitch rule to serve only ten years for this gruesome murder she helped commit.

Live your beliefs and you can turn the world around.

—Henry David Thoreau

Knuckie took medication for a while after her son's death. The doctor wanted her to continue to take meds, but Knuckie refused.

She became ferocious toward everything and everyone. The five-hundred dollars in insurance money from her son's death was gone. She had no other money other than mother's she was stealing on a regular basis. She needed to emotionally compensate for her grief; the only material things she had were free gifts and her car, for which she paid cash.

One day, as I returned home from an out-of-town salon, I got a call. It was my attorney, whom I retained because of the Knuckie mess. In disbelief, I slid to the floor. I wanted to kill myself.

My sister seemed to be a vengeful demon bent on hurting me and my children. She did not want me around to outshine her. Mother always looked at me as a diamond. Mom said to me on her deathbed she did not know why Knuckie did not like either of us. To this day, I am perplexed.

Knuckie spirit rang loudly in my spirit to tend to her. I went back and forth about how she have mistreated me lied on me and sent me to prison. I did not feel any love for her at all. I ask God to forgive my lack of compassion for her.

There were two relatives who dealt with Knuckie residing with her a few years. She would call the authorities whenever she did not get her way with them to try to put them out. Finally, the moment came that one of the relatives moved out. The situation became superheated.

Our first cousin Peete got involved. Growing up, Peete and I were best friends, but he wore on my trust. He would tell everyone about others and their business for sport, but he never shared his own. It was Peete who allied himself with Knuckie. I knew he would cause more trouble, so I paid a friend to pick him up to help with Mom and be around family.

Even still, Peete signed and was mentioned in all Knuckie's police reports. I knew I would not ever be able to trust Peete again. At times, I confronted Peete, and I meant it when I told him he acted out of vindictiveness. I knew both he and my sister well, so I decided, unless they changed, there wouldn't be much love or any trust for either of them in the future.

Knuckie had a plan. A perpetually self-entitled person. She would see to it her, and Peete did everything in their power to steal from one another believing I would have walked away with everything. They betrayed me behind my back to my mother taking advantage of the sickly. Today Knuckie is sickly with so many terminal illnesses and her new boyfriend now married steals everything he could from her. They both received their karma.

In between relationships and many affairs, Knuckie often found herself broke and ill. Unemployed and out of people to steal from, Knuckie relied entirely on the $500,000 insurance payout. At the rate she spent, however, she would not have money in twenty-two months. This is what the current boyfriend did not know.

She did not have a house of her own or any property other than her car. My sister descended into loneliness. Following her son's death, she resolved not to enter a relationship for eight years.

Then, she met Banker. Tall, slender, well-groomed, and educated, Banker hustled for his money. He was an ambitious entrepreneur—a self-made millionaire. Everything he claimed as his he schemed to acquire. He owned his own insurance agency and supermarket, wrote exclusive policies, and invested wisely. He was a family insurance agent to whom many referred friends and relatives, and so he was reasonably wealthy. He took advantage of his clients who sought a relationship; he supported them with insurance policies. If they ran short of funds, Banker would extend his hands. He gave his clients loans on their policies. Then they became his slaves.

Knuckie always told me when Banker visit mom's home he like me as a person. "You're smart" he said. Unlike my sister. I communicated intellectually, a fact that wounded her pride. As an adult, Knuckie boyfriends respected me for my intelligence and perspective. He always wanted to have me around when he visited Mom's house with whom Knuckie resided with her for thirty-five years. This is yet no reason to want everything Mother has just because you found herself broke in twenty-one months having a half of a million dollars or even residing in mother's home I quick claim to mother and Knuckie swindled it out of her, telling her she's going do for her when she received her life insurance policy and did nothing for her. Knuckie did for Banker more than she would ever do for her mother. She was just a big o'l sucker for him and he liked men. Boi' was he sly. He was after nothing more than to squirrel her money from her.

Dennis, her boyfriend now crack-smoking husband in jail again was not at all attractive. I did not know how she ever picked these guys up forget what she seen in them. She was blinded by their attention. I can see how Banker played his cards with her on a business deal nothing more.

My sister believed everything he told her as if nothing was wrong with this fella. He had three daughters all three had the same birthday and year. She seen him as a professional. He sold insurance. Some seen him as a hustler and a thief.

I doubt Banker was attracted to my sister. He was out to get what he came for. And this was to contribute to his bank account for himself. They never expressed any interest in one another. I notice only in men which he had around, and they were always gay. I find some gay men very selective, observant, smart, intelligent, and creative all the good qualities one with class would like. Banker had a lot of class a big baller, broker, entrepreneur and very savvy. Knuckie spent money with Banker every chance she could.

After about two years, she settled for Dennis – who recently been ejected from his mother's house and who habitually disrespected, betrayed and beat women. She thought he had income she told me, and he thought she had more of the half million dollars. Banker was not trying to allow anyone to get a flinch of that dough she had. When Banker bounced, she did not have much of anything remaining. He did not want her thinking he came and ran, which he did. Dennis preyed on Knuckie to support himself a total bum.

Knuckie constantly went to the hospital by ambulance. The woman whom Knuckie put out the house who resided with her for a few years once married to our cousin Peete leaving the premises, not giving her ample time to find a place. Her new crack-headed boyfriend did not want her to see how he abused her. He would have been in prison much sooner beating Knuckie if she would have stayed. He did not want anyone to see all he did there. He punched holes in the doors and wall of the house, he stole all of her and Mother's jewelry. Sick once again, Knuckie stayed in the ICU for six weeks. We only knew learned of it by way of other relatives, and not her new live-in boyfriend who had taken her cellphone, car, and house keys. He partied with other women in the home. They both had the family fooled.

At one point, her boyfriend went to jail for violating a restraining order with two separate girlfriends. Now awaiting his release, Knuckie had us over to the house. I n laughter, she rambled about how she received gifts and money from those who thought she and Dennis married. They received gifts and money and thought it was funny to actually take advantage of others because they both were unable to pay for a justice of the peace and the marriage license so they pretend to be until eighteen months later they made it official.

Knuckie end up in the hospital again. I only knew because one of my sons witnessed the paramedics take her away on a stretcher from her home again. Now we are speaking for the first time in four years. I called Knuckie back to see what it is she wanted with me. Although her behavior was so blatant everyone in her periphery noticed it. I forgave her and went to care for her. I could have yet my heart is soft reflecting back on how she has mistreated me, and the only other feeling would have been hatred for her. I did not allow for my heart or mind to go there. God was melting all the unbearable pain I had endured coming from her.

Over the phone, she asked, "Would you come live with me"? I'm behind on bills".

No way, I thought. I could not believe she needed me so desperately. Guilt weighing on my conscience. Mother did tell us to love one another and be there for one another was all I thought of, knowing we all we have and not everyone is able to understand life and childhood issues that most people do not know exist in their lives that they ignore and some battle. I berated myself. I talked To God, tears flowing I confided in Him. I felt bound to her madness. My daughter Lala begged me repeatedly to visit her. We had long difficult conversations. I thought I should be there for my sister. Inclined to indulge her I ask if anyone else would live there. I am thinking in grace although she is unworthy, I am going to do it if I could. If she needs me. I seen that she was only out to get her bills paid any way she could. I did not feel up to being used in my face from someone who could not ever be worth it for me. She replied and said her boyfriend not really wanting to say. She was not certain if I would ask all the right questions to have her answer me directly. She replied saying her boyfriend. I immediately said no way will I be caring for any man, especially a bum, you got to be kidding me. And the thing about it she knows he's a bum and would like for me to care for both. She has no morals neither does he looking for a way out.

We visited her at the hospital once, where Knuckie told me she would soon be discharged and asked if she could call me.

"Yes, no problem," I replied. I did not know what she wanted or what she was up to. I knew it was something pertaining to money; during this time, she struggled with her income. Her social security had been downsized because of where she was working and hadn't reported her earnings. She didn't have the foresight to think if her lies would catch up with her. Her only concern was keeping her man and his only concern was money.

Over the phone, as expected, Knuckie told me she was behind on her taxes and bills. She wanted to me take over the house.

"No way," I emphatically told her. I had just been injured on the job and was moving from a high-end, rat-infested townhouse in the city. The prospect of yet more problems overwhelmed me. It was also upsetting that she had the nerve to burden me with her turmoil. Still, I didn't want her to lose the house, so I asked my oldest daughter if she would consider moving in with Knuckie.

My daughter told me, "No, and don't ask me again."

Knuckie's boyfriend had lied to her regarding his incarceration, including what he had done and what his charges were. In any case, she did not have the money to bail him out.

After he served his time, it did not take long for authorities to arrest him again. This time, his probation issued a warrant against him for violation of probation, often abbreviated as VOP. The more Knuckie discovered about her boyfriend, the more she lied to us. She said he could not come back because she was done with him. She has said anything for someone to care for her now she has a handicap.

Two weeks later, Knuckie allowed us to pack his clothes and bring them all to his mother's house. Everyone knew it was a façade. Even her best friend, who was also her physical therapist, knew he'd come home to a free ride. He would call her frequently. All along, we took excellent care of her, and she took advantage of us.

She realized I had to go home to tend to my own affairs, but she did not want me to leave her home at all. Why would she, when I was spending money on groceries for her despite her freezers being full of food? I did not care to cook or prepare any meals, so I bought things for her as well as for my daughter and grandkids. This is how life goes.

We had other relatives come over and stay the night to help her. That was a blessing. Knuckie's nurse and physical therapist got involved because they knew he had beaten and physically abused her. She was telling us stories about it. I recorded her and shared it with her physical therapist, who always suspected the abuse.

She had not told them, but it was obvious. Broken fixtures, walls, and doors littered the house. I once asked her who broke everything. Her answer was evasive. I couldn't believe what I saw or heard. Was she that desperate to have someone with her there? Was this what some men did to women to keep a roof over their heads? I'm certain he couldn't go back to live with any old girlfriend. Who wants to be bullied?

The moment I went home, I got a call from an unknown phone number. It was Knuckie. She accused three of us—her best friend, our cousin Gayle, and me—of stealing her credit cards and license from her coat. *Unbelievable.* The devil from the pit of hell working through my sister set me up again. This sort of tactic was common; in fact, she specialized in claiming theft. At this point, I was completely done.

Then, Knuckie told me everything her boyfriend did to her. He stole all of her and our mother's jewelry. I have her on recorder. He had broken her son's and his dad's pictures she kept on her armoire. He urinated on her.

This last one was hard to believe.

"Knuckie," I replied, my blood heating, "you lied to everyone and said *I* stole Mother's jewelry. Now, you sit here and tell me your boyfriend stole everything. You sent me to prison with lies; you got glory out of it."

She said, "No, I didn't." I could hear her sobbing, but I knew her well. Her tears were fake.

I yelled at her because she hadn't called the authorities on him at all. He violated every rule possible when it came to abuse, a crime especially heinous against a woman with a handicap. The only thing she said in response was she did not want to have him arrested.

But he beat her. Constantly. I know she was bored and lonely, but that is just stupid.

I had to go. I could not bare much of how I understood she never once loved me. Sometimes we have to bare the pain until it's no longer there. We must learn to forgive moved on let go and you tell yourself it's not your stuff to carry. I never once hit my sister. Although I was close to it. Mom stopped me a few times. In other instances, Knuckie pulled the alarm in mother's home, so authorities would come to the house, and that was not any fun. It was chicken to alert the authorities when we argued. After a while, they would call first, to see if the alarm were accidental and Mother would say she was not paying two hundred dollars for anyone to come out.

The local authorities eventully knew Knuckie has deep rooted mental health issues. They see her issues each time they came out to the house she thought she had protection because she nearly told on anyone she could if they did not, please her. Before we lost Mother, Knuckie was diagnosed with cancer. She now needs a pacemaker and dialysis because her kidneys are in diabetic failure. She is all messed up with all sorts of terminal illnesses, her karma.

Eventually, she located her credit cards and license, but she never once called me or anyone back to say she found them. My daughter had to call to inform me.

When you get like this—vindictive and desperate—you fight away people who love you and want to help sustain you. I had to learn the devil can no longer fool me. It may disguise itself, but it uses the same tactics, and it is the same story. I had never once ever thought my sister or myself are not friends never thought it would ever happen. This is when we must decide who we are going to live for. The devil would fathom harming God's children. It is up to you to decide if you would like to deal with the devil or choose to be smart. The devil only comes to kill steal and destroy.

It was hard to care for her. Whenever I was home, I'd find the time to dwell on it and didn't want to ever return. Now, I'm so glad I did it all out of love. I found myself crying to God about it. The Bible tells us our foe is within our own household. We must be careful of nothing but submit everything to God in prayer. I'm only sharing this drama because I must be honest. It's not about hurting her. It's about giving God the glory and sharing His work. There is no one who is exempt from any sort of trouble in this world. There is strife in every race and in every denomination. For me, it's a spiritual warfare. I am highly favored!

I walk alone. I have been misunderstood because of who I am, despised, and rejected by someone who should love me. I must pray these demons get off me. They are mad I'm back in God's grace and glory.

I did not understand how God allowed Knuckie to get away with all she did to others and me. Today, karma has caught up with her. I do not wish her any harm, but I realize God will punish those who deserve it. He uses good and evil to accomplish what He promised. When I look back on my life, I realize God poured out His oil over me. To God be the glory! Through Him, all the struggles, grief, and poor choices in my past will make sense.

I worked hard to care for her. She is lazy and overweight. I realized she has an eating demon; all she wants to do is eat with a hangdog face all day long saying she is hungry. She burns me out with her stress, drama, and chaos. We as people work twice as hard to save those who are troubled while we reckon with our own difficulties. I am energized and motivated to fight for people who remind me of me. We must put things behind us, so we do not use today's strength on yesterday's battle. As a younger person, I collapsed, cried, and screamed. Logically, others expected me to continue my downward trajectory. God, however, changed my attitude to turn my life around. I'm going to praise Him because I'm receiving the victory.

I laid hands on Knuckie firsthand to pray for her at her request. This evening I observed Knuckie watching me. She did not wish for me to leave until I prayed the faith of prayer over her. All day we laughed and smiled together, yet I noticed how Knuckie was feeling sorry for herself or planning for my life once she knew I wasn't staying. I assured her I will be there for her no matter what. I continued to come by to care for her as her boyfriend ends up in jail for two weeks. During this time his probation had come to an end. The dept of corrections did not do their job again. She knows I am anointed, a child of God, have the anointing, gifted, talented and bless enough to where she needs to be able to trust someone and the trust is not there in the home.

What she would have done to keep me in her presence any and everything as she had tried too.

She knows I have the power to do within myself through the anointing of The Holy Spirit that dwells within me. She said she felt something leave her body and the home. It had to go. What I am saying is this Knuckie knows I am powerful. She wanted her moment with me letting me know she is now sick being told sad news in and out of the hospital. She realizes she need to tell her sister what's going on with her somehow without feeling inadequate about being in her presence, after doing me so wrong, not knowing how I was going to accept her being she went out her way twice to contact me. It was important to her because I had stop dealing with her for some time but not too long.

This is my life story, and this is my song. I will not stop playing it. God is working all things after the counsel of His own will. If it had been for the pain, I would not have the power. If I had not had the problem, I would not have the promise. I worship you Jesus. I have been through too much not to lift my hands and worship Him. I have no room for distractions. Because of my sacrifice, people will remember me.

During my last stay in prison, I learned to lean on God for everything. He showed me my life is in His hands. I could do nothing more than educate myself while I was there. The rage and lack of forgiveness towards Knuckie vanished. I refuse to be taken up by vultures as I live life. I had to realize her behavior remained the same no matter how well I treated her. As a young lady, I did not know how to deal with it. I would cry, argue and talk smack. I did not want to be this kind of person to her or anyone else, whether I am in or out of prison. I love God – He is the God of love.

Never did I dare imagine this kind of relationship with my sister. I remember sisters from different families who had issues and they did not get along maybe only in front of others. I was unable to phantom pretending we as sisters did not have any family issues among ourselves. I did not see it until we were much older. They were not my issues her issues alone. I just could not understand how and why she felt the way she did about me and why, no matter what she told me. I never went after any of her boyfriends. I would not. I could still distance myself and do what I need to do for my happiness. I had to cut the cord of discord between my sister and me. I refuse to be in a situation where a person struggles with either themselves or their life projects their unhappiness onto me.

Church

*I may not have gone where I intended to go, but I think I have
ended up where I intended to be.*

—Douglas Adams

MY GRANDMOTHER ALWAYS ENVISIONED HERSELF running
a church with all her grandchildren. The Lord instructed her on how to build
a family church. First, she needed money. She sent her grandchildren, including myself, to request a building fund from various towns. My grandmother
obtain permits from every town we solicited in. When we rang doorbells to
solicit for contributions, we even came across some of our schoolteachers. We
were always getting treats; people would give us a cold glass of water, mints,
cookies, or fruit when they gave a contribution. Then, they would sign their
name on a sheet with how much they gave. We would get a daily incentive
per dollar amount we brought in.

She spoke the building into existence. Through determination and the
Lord's guidance, she became a founder.

My grandmother would bring us to knock on doors two or three times
a week. We enjoyed it. Afterwards, she would bring us to get something from
McDonald's or Howard Johnson's Restaurant.

Anywhere we went, I would always encounter someone who quietly
asked me if one of my parents was white. When they asked which one, I would
lie and say it was my dad. I have green eyes, which appear blue or gray when
I wear different clothing or even as my mood changes. Although my father

the only sibling with green eyes and curly hair. We all inherited his eyes. He was not light-skinned like me. I inherited his hustling habit as well as his involvement in organized crime.

During my childhood, I believed so strongly I would be just like my dad. All his clothing came from Stagpole & Moore Clothier, a high-end clothier in existence for at least eighty years. I shopped at same store as my dad in the seventies and eighties. I admired everything about my dad's lifestyle—except when he cheated on our mother. As soon as I turned twenty years old, I began buying banker-style corporate skirts—old, conservative, long, pleated skirts—and non-wrinkle white blouses from Stagpole & Moore's.

I began shopping for myself at the age of fifteen. My mother would always buy my school clothes from Weathervane. Mom spend two-hundred and fifty dollars on me for school shopping. I always had to have more. I would do what I knew—I shopped using someone else's money or credit card. I enjoyed what I did hustling getting arrested did not phase me until you realize it gets tiresome when you looked over your life and see you're not where you ever thought you would be in your life. I discovered in my circle of people I know never arrested and commit crimes daily to get ahead. Perhaps only because haven't been arrested for anything. My mother was my enabler. She felt responsible for what I knew and saw from my father's lifestyle. I wanted what he had for myself—nothing more. I did not know what he did as a hustler until many years later. I wanted to emulate it.

I now know this is not a good mindset for any child. Children are innocent, and when a parent cannot control or change their behavior, he or she negatively influences them. Parents have their own issues and don't always know how to make changes to their own situation.

Mom would constantly ask what activities I wanted to do. As our primary caretaker, she kept us productive with gymnastics, piano lessons, modeling school, camp, and more. From the age of five to thirteen, she'd ask what I'd like to do when I grew up. I would say, "I wanna be just like my dad."

I also told Mother I wanted to be the world's top model as I was older. She later enrolled me in the Barbizon Modeling School for classes. The makeup artists painted my face until I looked like JonBenét. As a kid, I didn't like the rouge on my cheeks or the red lipstick on my lips. I was only eleven years old. This is what they wanted me to wear while there and when I left to go home, but I just wasn't feeling the look at all. My Mom did everything in her power to keep me on track.

I was in the Revitalization Corp an after-school program for kids. There were volunteers who helped school-aged children with their homework. They taught us how to play guitar, read stories, do arts and crafts, and just had a good ol' fun time. I worked with Project COOP at age ten. As for those in the program we would receive eighty dollars weekly until the end of the summer. Our final check for two-hundred dollars last day.

I worked summer jobs with the elderly for CRT at the Norris Grave Senior Apartment Living in the Rec Department. I was selected to attend Ethel Walker School, a preparatory girl's school for the Sphere Summer Program. I learned to appreciate various kinds of activities I did not get to experience in urban areas such as macramé, volleyball, and campfires. The camp counselors had us sit in a circle while they told incredible stories. We would ask questions, and they would improvise answers.

If you don't have a sense of self-worth, it doesn't matter how many accolades people throw at you.

—Gugu Mbatha-Raw

To dream is to think beyond what's shown to you. Push beyond what you have been taught.

—Afua Richardson

Life leads us to unexpected places. At about age seventeen, I let a sergeant in the U.S. Army National Guard talk me into enlisting. Underage and just given birth to my first child my oldest son. I could not go without permission. Mom agreed, and in I was. I gave birth four months later and left my baby behind. Back in my high school, cliques of young girls aligned themselves for a sense of belonging. As a teenager, I did not fit in. I yearned to do something entirely different in my life for a greater cause.

The army flew me to For Jackson, South Carolina for boot camp. At the receptionist station, officials interviewed me and taken my photo in standard-issue uniform complete with a dickie and hat. Nowadays, I wish I had that picture.

Afterward they asked if my parents went to court for custody of my child. Bells noisily rang in my psyche. Why would they ask this? Did they expect my parent to seize custody? The gentlemen documenting my answers told me I would be given a DD214. What does that mean? What's a DD214.

"What does this mean? What is a DD214?"

"In the event of an honorable discharge," he replied simply, "do you want to return?"

Immediately, I nodded my head – all while I knew I was lying. I told my inner spirit, When I get out of here, I'll never return.

Within the first few days after getting situated, we were given assignments. Hungry child molesters all around the camp took advantage raping the young teens. These were not men sneaking onto base – they were the officers of the government. Relief swept over me on the plan ride home after being handed a DD214 honorable discharge.

One of the benefits of military service includes a membership with the USAA Bank works exclusively with currents and former military forces as well as their families. After my discharge, I wanted products and services with the bank but could not be verified for credit. Only years later I discovered why. While examining my official military document, I noticed my date of birth was incorrect. The date was for someone three years older than me. Realization, decades in the making, hit me. I made the appropriate phone calls to the State Armory. I waited and watched from a distance as the service-member removed and entered my new data, to correct my birthdate. Today,

I use a copy of the updated information for any and everything I can. I take pride in my service, as the people in our military have earned it. Perhaps if I were much older or mature, I would have pursued the myriad of benefits the military offers. Then, it would have been a good career.

However, I witnessed terrible acts from men bearing medals of honor. Even their peers know, but no one says anything. To think—parents' children enlist in the hopes they'll make a difference. Yet, the government fosters and protects pedophiles in their ranks who train your child, and it's kept quiet. I made a mistake not returning. I was not ready for the treatment I saw there. It looked and felt like prison. I had not been to prison this time in my life. It was all in what I experienced and witnessed there. The situation hasn't improved. Pedophiles wield tremendous power in this country, including Harvey Weinstein, Jeffrey Epstein, and too many others to mention.

The best way to make tomorrow better is to do something better today. If not, tomorrow will be no different. Those mired in their choices believe their past and future are the same, and so they live as if no change is possible. I will run this race. My past is not my future.

For from within, out of a person's heart, come evil thoughts, sexual immorality, theft, murder, adultery, greed, wickedness, deceit, lustful desires, envy, slander, pride, and foolishness. All of these vile things come from within; they are what defile you.

—Mark 7:21-23 (NLT)

What the enemy conspires against me will fail; no weapon formed against me shall prosper. True deliverance comes with honesty and compassion, not perfection. This story serves to help those searching for answers in their walk with God. It is for those who mask their sins in order to call themselves Christians. You can keep that title for a long time and not know much of anything.

God is omniscient. He allows others to hurt so you know he or she is not your friend. You will know you're ready to inhabit what God has for you when people in your past want you back. You need to know there's a blessing in the enemies' camp whether you suffer for four or fourteen years. My disobedience towards God was the problem. Through every trauma, trial, crime, and conviction, I have learned I was built to help someone else. Sin must be addressed, if not forgiven.

I have yet to do God's will in the face of my enemies under pressure, but seasons always change the situation. I am a wealthy woman waiting on my money. I have been pushed to the place I'm currently in. I will not impress broke folks. I will not involve myself with folks without anything to their name, and who feel threatened by someone with more. Some trials demand a testimony of your faith.

Something almost killed me fourteen years ago. What kills the average person strengthens those of us who are chosen. When it happened to me, I trusted God and encouraged others. It was when I discouraged myself that I backslid and reverted to intentionally acting in my old ways. I had to be infected by sin to be effective. My illness could not be rebuked; I had to live through it. There was no demon; God would have told it to leave me. Just because terrible things happen does not mean a devil is present. I was low in funds because He wanted more of me. He creates problems just for me. When you praise God and do not give credit to the devil, you see a challenging experience on the horizon.

The issues I faced were not after my life. They got what they came for—money and time. They did not get me. My money barred me from Jesus just as not having money brought me to Jesus. He sent a storm to get me back. No demons lurked in any of the storms. I was the highest low-cast woman in the Bible to get to Jesus.

You cannot cover illness with clothes or dress up a personal flaw. What you cover you cannot cure. The more money I had, the more luxury surrounded and suffocated me.

The gospel is not for us to hide behind, and it does not perfect us. It exists to elevate our awareness of our actions and our lives—to embarrass us into change. Some people say, when you are chosen, you convict yourself. Chosen folks, however, do not embody the same rules. The intensity of this self-chastisement is wrong. The way I spank my daughter is different from how I spank my son. We must preach it right even though we live it wrong. Anyone who claims perfection lies. My perspective is my lens on life.

These issues originate in my family, even in the relatives I never met. They travel through the blood. I came to believe my story resonates with the stories of many women. This narrative will tell you who I am. I attribute no fault to anyone but myself. As people, we need to learn about ourselves, make changes, and not blame anyone for anything. In other words, if I backslide the progress I've made, I might slip into old habits and lose my motivation. Negative viewpoints might seep in; I might become fearful when I should be courageous, insecure instead of confidant, suspicious instead of trusting, and I might give up instead of persisting. Negativity fails to solve our problems, yet our struggles grant us an opportunity to make progress. A positive mind notices opportunity for progress, while a negative one closes itself to possibilities.

Some of us were just never taught or never learned how to practice constructive thinking. Yes, my parents and grandparents told me moralistic stories, and yes, they were good stories, but they fell short of realistically addressing the challenges we face as adults. We only see the dirty stuff as we get older and understand reality is not anything like the stories we were told.

Despite what I've lost—despite what has slipped out of my hands—God hasn't changed His mind about me. God teaches me to hold on to what He has given me. After years of struggle, I arrived at a place of transformation—a place where change comes hand selected from our Lord. People can only change when they walk away from their backgrounds. It is a challenging thing to do; we sometimes are loyal to what is wrong. My family dynamic, our DNA, and family patterns are part of who I am. I'm aware I lived a life of hardship and self-destruction, but I didn't know it would affect an innocent child. I did whatever I need to do, whether it was right or wrong, to survive. That said, I also acted out of hunger for the material world.

If God grants fruits in life, he also creates challenges. In the moment of those challenges, God allowed me a choice. I could not claim to be good if I have never been tempted to be bad. All temptation begins within us and always follows the same patterns—a desire becomes a thought, which becomes action through disobedience and deception of others. If I did not have the internal desire, the temptation would not attract me. It starts in the mind, not in the circumstances. On many occasions, the thoughts play repeatedly in my mind. This is what begins as an idea, then births into behavior. Finally, I gave into what got my attention. I was tempted to do what I thought when trapped by my own evil desires, then my evil desires conceived and gave birth to sin. Every time I attempted to ignore thoughts to commit a crime, I drove them deeper into my mind until I acted on them. The more I fought the feeling, the more it consumed me.

Today, I know how to change my mindset. I learned to set loose the negativity. The Bible tells us that our cry for God's grace will be heard because Jesus is sympathetic to us. The temptation in my life is no different from what others experience. I am focusing all my energy on forgetting the past and looking forward to what lies ahead. God can do for us more than we would ever dare to ask or even dream of.

My story is one of the causes and effects of diseases. I often think of how, like the forensic study of disease, a clear mechanism for the problem emerges through examination. I discovered from both my parents and their parents how and why things are the way they are in my life.

The disease I discovered in my bloodline is called cancer. I am not talking about the colon cancer that killed my mother or the prostate cancer that killed my dad nor the cancers that killed both my maternal and paternal grandparents. The disease I discovered in my life experience was a powerful cancer demon—the root of all evil. Mental, emotional, and behavioral disorders infected the foundation of my life. I repeated both my parents' mistakes in my relationships. From one generation to the next, beliefs and patterns were passed down to me. As a result, we've lived our lives plagued by diminished self-worth and low self-esteem.

To discover who I am, I liberated my inner child. I reminded myself of what it is to think positively and see the world with fresh eyes.

Reflection, understanding, and purposeful action take effort, time, and discipline. It surprises me how much I have already learned—and how I constantly learn more—about myself. When we self-reflect, we understand ourselves. We feel most spirited, authentic and genuine. My true self is compassionate and generous without fear or judgement. He accept us and others just the way we are. I've grown up without realizing my needs have never been met, which is one reason I lived unhappy and confused for so long.

Anything I did not get from my parents they didn't get from theirs. They did the best they could. I understand that.

I grew up unprotected by my father. He was not there for me mentally or emotionally. Neither my parents nor my grandparents mistreated or abused me as a child.

Even in the absence of abuse, however, I still needed my father in my life daily, and I didn't get that. My mother frequently praised me such that I always looked for it from her. I knew when my father came to pay us a visit, he'd bring us a lot of money. We were able to spend it all on ourselves. We would go to concerts, buy sneakers and socks—whatever we wanted. This would have been in the 1960s. We always went out to dinner at restaurants, like IHOP, The Lobster Shack, The Brownstone, Captain Gallies, and Jimmy's. My parents always gave us nice treats.

My mother was many things: devoted, loyal, kind, patient, independent, assiduous, unselfish, and a deeply spiritual woman. My dad shared some of these traits; he was also self-reliant, giving, and a hard-worker, yet he was, at heart, a hustler. He steadfastly clung to resentment. My dad went to prison twice in my life. His second prison sentence took him away from us for twenty-one years of a fifteen- to thirty-year sentence. His first sentence was not as long—a few years if that. Drugs nor alcohol did not interest my parents. It would have taken them exceptionally more time to learn more about themselves; letting them know despite they are not drunks or addicts. They still have an addiction because of their behaviors and actions, opening to be more receptive. learning who they are. It hurts to see when we miss things that could have made a significant difference in our lives. If he knew what I know today about his addiction as a hustler someone who did not know he had an addiction would have him startled. He would not be able to do it all alone. I was unable to do it all alone, to get to one step and just knowing. I learned only by listening and believing in those who spoke their truth without hiding anything. He was blinded by knowing that his addiction is cunning baffling and powerful something I had refuse to believe and did not understand it in my life. I see he noticed at a late age before his death he accepted Jesus as his lord and savior. Our addictions are nothing we could rid of on our own. It takes the help of Jesus Himself to intervene all powerful and all knowing He has the power to do all things but fail.

Although my father also was a trailer truck driver, transport modular homes to their destination. As a kid I had a lot of questions for dad as to where he gets his money. I knew or at least speculated his employer did not pay him all the earnings he has. Curious and inquisitive what parent would give their children all of their pay at one time. I wanted to know why he is living with a woman and yet still married to our mom. Every day, I watched my mother grow more tired of the façade. Then, she got married to a man from Jamaica, had a baby with him. And yet, she never let go of the love she had for Dad. In their late seventies they spent their last ten years on earth together. That shows the extent of their love for each other.

God extends blessings to all of us, but when we fail to forgive, we cannot receive them. As my dad grew older, he realized he needed to forgive to accept his blessing. Dad let go of any resentment or shame to get some peace.

I inherited much of who I am from my mother, who in turn inherited those same characteristics from her mother my grandmother. We all share the same fierceness of loyalty and devotion to others. But, as much as we are who we need to be for others, were also tenaciously independent. I invented rules to survive. What I needed to do to get by informed my own code of morals.

I escaped repercussion for all I taken. And my daughter stories are much like mine. When I recognize the patterns in my life, I felt a sensation I had not before – victimhood. I felt like a victim for the first time in my life of crime. I learned with every credit card I used without permission and with every fraudulent scheme, I made both conscious and unconscious decisions grounded in pathology. Some of that pathology my father passed to me, and some I created through a lifetime of trauma and choices.

Revenge was served cold while anger still burned. Mann's killers planned for payback when he least expected. The plan however quickly turned sour.

Charles my nephew who we called Mann was a devoted person well round savvy businessperson who attend Morehouse College and Arizona State. Also, a great athlete. He attended school in Simsbury all his younger years from first grade to twelfth. He wore Louis Vuitton shoes, drove a 760 BMW drop-top convertible and resided in a suburban neighborhood with his young children. The thugs in town resented what he had. The greasy, slime-bucket lowlifes could only afford the hood, lived with their family or with girlfriends on Section 8.

The family of the foul maggots who conspired in my nephew's murder relative shot my son in two thousand and eighteen. My son someone who's not a troublemaker can hold his own in a fight knew how to fight. As a kid he learned karate, kickboxing, taekwondo, sports and gymnastics so fighting is not an issue for him. He enjoyed fighting matter of fact to prove he could. His friends he grew up with loves him because they knew how to or would learn something they challenged. The siblings and cousin of Fly the maggot who setup my nephew Mann. A hating close friend who acquainted himself among the posse felt inadequate. Mann punked him a couple of times as he held onto it in his feelings forever until it involved him to set him up. The solution was to rob and kill, get a gun and run. They knew they had to kill him out of fear nothing more.

While my son fights for his life in the hospital ER. I thought the worst. When I arrived, there were folks pretending to be his mom telling a false story it occurred over some chaos over his girlfriend which was not true. The informant sister felt inadequate because she had been intimidated and thought she could handle something having a big head. I was told by my son. The detective told me his condition was stable. The bullet pierced his armpit. It came out within three centimeters of his heart.

He refused to cooperate with the police. The authorities – one local cop and federal agent – spoke to me to gather information and for me to pressure my son, neither of which would happen. The particularly nasty officer was pissed because my son told them both to get the fuck out of his room as he did pushups. with a shrug, the officer said unless my son was willing to cooperate, there was nothing they could do. The department had a clear footage and a photo of the person, asking if I knew him the shooter. The other assailants who also fled in their mother's vehicle were Fly brother and two of his sisters driving their mothers white Acura SUV. They knew they were not made up to do any prison bids, did not have it in them scary, is why they ran. The officers ask if I knew him the shooter who shot and ran. I told the officers I did not know any of his siblings. I did not know them from a can of paint. Likewise, my son did not know any of them other than Fly sisters. There were witnesses who out there who did, some stopped me to tell me they witnessed it. The officers inly involved me in case my son passed away. I watched the footage. The officers knew who they are. I knew either the authorities would get the assailant, or they would get it.

Once my son was discharged same night, he gave me the facts. The ones who fired the shots jumped into the mother's vehicle, then all four sped off. These were young kids who were trying to make a rap for themselves by shooting and running, that's no fun. I wanted vengeance on all of them.

The police knew these people. They were informants. The authorities knew this case was not going to be in my sons favor because he's not a rat he holds his own.

      I tried contacting one of the mothers who children were participants in this, who I grew up with in Bellevue Square. I begged her to gather the group of them and tell them to stop the madness with her children. She totally ignored me; matter of fact she had the authorities come to my residence saying how I harassed them. On other hand when the officers arrived, I just came in from working construction did not expect them, but I did because of who I am and who my family is. I forgot they have my residence address which I gave when I was approached at the hospital ER my info, nothing I would have done voluntarily on my own. Upon arriving at my door, they knew it was more to it, they were not just taking one side of the story. Listening to what brought them to my residence I let it be known I'm not a happy mother learning my son was shot and the assailant the authorities knew who he was, and all who were involved. Immediately after saying what all, I had to say I showed the two officers the statements the daughter had sent me on messenger "your son gets what he gets" and other contributing factors of their guilt! it proved her involvement their guilt of all they knew about the case. The officers pulled out their cell phones taken pictures of the messages as well as what I said begging the mom to stop her children from this madness. I knew there were going to be furthermore problems down the road with this. My son would not have no dealings with the authorities. The detectives were skeptical it would be further retribution. A homicide detective who led the case in my nephew's case called my phone leaving voice mail saying," talk to my son so there would not be any retribution". They felt it was further from over.

They knew they started an unwinnable fight. No One was ever visible. No one who hides is innocent. There was talk on the street the police placed them in safe houses for their protection.

Fly, the betrayed friend informant who set up my nephew's murder has been released now from prison after serving two years with his cooperation. Most of the cowards begin to snitch on one another fearing they could not do much prison time. Fly uncles who are in law enforcement helped him reach his freedom having him snitch on as many as he could for his freedom. Some of them snitched on a bank robbery they committed for leniency in this case. Fly now being out no more than a year, nearly died sitting in his car in a parking lot o a hot summer day. Fly claimed he never knew his friends planned to murder Man. Once out of federal prison, he forgot what he did. The feds also know those types of informants do not last long out on the streets. Fly thought informants were safe. Yet the feds dispose of them. Now a days snakes and rats get more recognition for their loyalty of being who they are.

One day, my sister got a surprise visit from a friend, who told her the guy who set up her son's murder was killed. He had sat at a carwash, unassuming, when the bullets punctured his car into his body where he was at and what he had done. Many celebrated the end of this chapter. However, it was not the case. A hospital was right across the street from the carwash, a coincidence which saved his life. I do not wish death on anyone, yet some people deserve to die. He went on Facebook after this incident, cowardly saying, Fuck you. He was partially paralyzed.

The relatives of Fly who shot at my son, their family home had been shot up and someone had some bullet scares. They had to be fled out of their home by EMT's. On my way home one weekend there were traffic I decided to take a detour and notice as I passed by ambulances and police cruisers. Some came out on stretchers.

The government, meanwhile, always tries to have it their way. I do not care about any federal organization, agent or anyone else. If they were to decide to hold me without bail, I would not fear what they could do being I did nothing wrong, someone else on the other hand would tell on anyone to get out just for the moment and not care who they told on.

The judicial system is dirty. I wish I filmed the first day at the Rentschler Field Stadium in East Hartford. The entire Hartford Police Department retirees attended. I My jaw dropped. I forgot I was at work. I lost interest in trying to get a football jersey from any player. These maggots were escorted shining as they walked their throne. I must say I was excited about what I witness about these retired officers in action as an adult. I recognized detectives who were then retired who would be in the field when I was hustling. They are officers who had a stench expression on their face that told they were a cop distinctively and basically got informants to do their job. Every person wore clothing I associated with gangsters – cashmere coats hung from their shoulders, Homburg hats sat atop of their heads, and their hands gripped expensive canes. Bodyguards stood stoically at their employer's side. I was working there hoping to get a football jersey from any player missing the time they would come out of their dressing room, just to watch these gangsters. When I say the entire Hartford Police Department as indistinguishable from all kinds of people professed were criminals. I forgot all about the jerseys. Scenes like this set off a trigger within me.

We all saw a criminal activity in the White House. The administration of the forty-fifth president stunk with corruption. Officials took advantage of the minority groups and sent them away to prison. Prolonged prison time keeps Black people impoverished. Certain friend of the former president as well as the former President Donald Trump has been claimed to have raped more women which could have brought up on charges like Bill Cosby and R. Kelly handed a sentence which only Black people are handed for such charges. Forget ever being arrested for any. With impunity, the system allowed these creatures to walk free because they have money. I will never trust another white man in power who holds an official position. Imagine a mobster twirling a coin between his fat fingers—These are the figures in our government. Did we, as African Americans, really need a president such as Trump leading our country? His actions toward minorities proved he is a racist. He allowed for others not to hide their own bigotry. He played an enormous role in every problem our country has. He profited at our expense. He downplayed and failed to act on a global pandemic, which, as a result, exacerbated the situation, and he did so to win reelection. Mr. Trump even stated what he would do to the country if he did not win. He knew he was losing and so did he loose.

Trump's greatest fear was having President Biden and VP Harris (who is the first African American woman in her role) in charge of *his* country. To have this duo succeed him is an embarrassment to Trump. He degraded them at every opportunity. When recounts failed to deliver him a victory, what did he do? He called on his supports, some of whom were occult leaders or part of violent militant groups, and incited insurrection of the United States Capital. What was more, the government enabled him. He acted with impunity. I believe those who voted to acquit him in both his impeachments were paid.

My family has its political connections! My great-great-aunt's son Joseph Rainey, who had just bought his freedom, became the first person born from a slave family to serve in the House of Representatives. His district elected him in the South Carolina during Reconstruction after the Civil War. Former slaves had just been affirmed their right to vote. Some of Joseph's greatest achievements including advocating for the rights of African Americans, Chinese Americans and Native Americans in the 1870's. He served four terms before segregationist laws across the south forced him and another blacks out of office. Seventy-years passed before another African American has represented the south in Washington.

A cousin from my father's side is a prosecutor in Jersey court, another cousin who is a doctor. Also, between my brother's daughters and my daughter are nurses in the family. My nephew Mann who was murdered only daughter a physical therapist. She switched her major along the way from nursing.

I am not a bad girl, far from it. I still have anger. It's justifiable. I do not believe there is anyone on this earth who is perfect or without sin except Jesus Himself. Despite the label affixed to me. I am not a flight risk.

I have sat in federal court too long – six years straight – before a judge sentence me. I have been around all types of people and none I trust. Any of them could kill. I know I'm capable of killing and could kill again. I had an abortion. At the time, I did what I needed to do to get rid of the fetus. The fact it could have become a child still weighs on me.

The five thugs who played a part in murdering my nephew are now captured. They all tried to play their best card – they cooperated being an informant on other people they acquainted themselves with in the hood fake friends huh. Only one dodged a life sentence, succeeded. There are those fellas who are afraid of placing a firearm in their hand to rob a bank and they will rob and murder a human being out of spite. For just a stick-up, they would receive ten to twenty years. Those five low life punk maggots killed my nephew, did not get any money, all but the one will die in prison. The other informant will have a rough time in hell on earth.

This is the highlights one's stupidity and laziness in how they obtain anything in life, and it tells me they do not deserve anything more than they have.

When it happened, both my brother Jerry and I were incarcerated. If we were free, we would have gone crazy in the night and killed if known who may have been involved. Jerry he would have done the most outrageous things to be done to anyone and the authorities knows this. God has held us in prison to feel the rage, pain and hurt and not act on it. I was stopped by a counselor in a women's prison to inform me I need to stick around because the police department would like to talk to me concerning a family member. I had a sad feeling it would not be good news and it wasn't. It was not the police but my only sister who have loss her only child to these low life maggots. The call came through and it was my sister she begins screaming saying they killed her son. I dropped the phone and ran down a long hallway nowhere to turn but to the cell. When they sent for me to go to the medical unit to speak to someone a therapist and perhaps medicate. I was allowed to make calls while there speaking to one of my younger sons who did not know any of this because he was in school. He was out of it when hearing the bad news taken it hard himself. Our family was close, and Mann was there for my children being I were in prison. I did not think to tell him when I did because children handle it differently than an adult would. I arrived back to my housing unit was receiving love from those who love me. I just could not go to sleep for four days exhausted and burned out being in a prison reliving what you may have thought happened and it continued to replay in your head, all I wanted to do is kill. It was so real. I almost lost it in the shower reliving it in my head for four days unable to sleep or find any rest. I was told that I would be given something that would allow for me to sleep. I had to follow directions from this medication and close my eyes to sleep in fifteen to thirty minutes because it had a window. I missed the window, but I do remember the first time getting a few hours of sleep that night, until I no longer wish to receive the meds. I had to deal with life as it came.

The difference between Jerry and myself he enjoyed television violent movies. I preferably did not care if I watched television or not. Jerry was seriously into violence with guns as a kid growing up watching the Wild Wild West. I did not have any favorites other than the Ranger Andy Show with other kids sitting with the ranger who read stories to the kids. I enjoyed watching the show so much, my mom had me on as a guest with the other kids one day. It was fun for me may have been five or six years old.

Jerry knew what it would take to get someone to give up their money. He tried it repeatedly. It became fascinating to him. Once a person knows how to envision it happening, they continue. We see all what our former president done as a persistent career criminal, never arrested for any of his stuff. It makes someone like me disliking those in power who allow this kind of behavior.

I later thank the Father He did not release me immediately after the shooting. Otherwise, I would have sought retribution on this family not caring who it harmed. Today I care about my life, my freedom, and love myself.

As for me violence has not ever been something I would like to be a part of, not to say I would not have killed. A killer kill and never stop no matter where they are. I Killed before, had an abortion, killed a fetus something I wanted no part of. It bothered me for a long time to where I had to deal with the Father about it in communicating to God. I made that choice without thinking long and hard about it. The decision I made as a teenager without my parent being involved, I made.

The strongest principle in growth lies in human choice.

—George Eliot

When I was eight years old, my mother's sister, a devoted Christian, was married to a king pin. Over the course of approximately twenty years a from (1950s to 1970s) they had everything they ever wanted and lost it all.

My mother loaned funds to save their properties. My mom's sister and her drug dealing husband did not have any intentions on repaying our mom a single mother of four money she saved through her employer. Mom had enough saved in her savings to buy a home for her four children she supported on her own was what she would be saving for. Mother decided to allow her sister and husband take out a loan believing they both would pay it back. It never happened. This tells you a lot about a person when they see you struggling and have children. They really don't care as long they get what they want. Mother said she wished she could have been more attentive having a lien placed on their property. The six thousand dollars was a lot for any single parent living in an apartment in the sixties. They also have assets. We learn as folks who have more than you and they need you financially will not return what it is they borrowed from an emergency. Its best not to give in believing because it looks a certain way doesn't mean they have it. People funds be all messed up and they will buy what they like and you will never know.

We often have neighbors who hang out and invite people over in the pool. As loaner I decide to play or be alone for most part unless I meet someone who I really enjoy playing with. I wanted to see what the other kids were doing being I knew they were in the neighbor's pool having a blast. I did not know how to swim. They had big fun diving into the pool and getting tossed in by Lori's father. They entire family knew how to swim. I decided to take a chance to go play with them at the pool. I walked a few doors down the street to one of the neighbors' homes. I noticed them in the back yard. I went to their front door. I could not see through their front door. I decided to let myself inside front door as I proceeded. I notice a glitch of sparkles shining as the ray of sun shadowing from a dresser. I walked over to it and seen it was a ring. I removed it from the dresser. It peeped my interest to my surprise it was a ring. I immediately removed it from their dresser exit back out the front door hoping no one see me leave out. I stole a diamond ring at eight nine years old to my surprise. Who places this much emphasis on thinking this way? I than wish to go in the house. I really did not feel up to playing really. I rang the doorbell at auntie's home, she answered by coming to the door. She may have been super bored.

She said, "Either you stay in or out, you're not going to be running in and out this door." To not hear what she has said to manipulate her "Look what I found" with my hand wide open. She forgot all she just said to me about running in and out. She removed the ring from my open hand and ask am I giving it to auntie as she removed it. I "nodded."

I did not know the value of it. I did know it had some value. Auntie lived extravagantly. She has a custom Eldorado Cadillac she drives to church. It stayed in the garage more than she drove it. When we did visit my brothers and I we played on their snow mobile, minibike, watched movies on their projector and ate snow cones on a regular. They had a huge ice machine in their basement. I stayed on the front steps until mom and grandma came to pick me up. Auntie did not tell my mom anything about the diamond she removed from my hand and kept.

On the car ride home mom had grandma turn the car around to go back to auntie's home being we had just pulled away two-hundred feet from her home. Mom went to ring the doorbell and ask auntie for the ring she removed from my hand. Auntie immediately said, she gave it to me", mom said," she did not "auntie would not give the ring to mom. Mom entered back into the car to proceed to go home. Mom and grandma was talking about it. I turned my ear from listening to their conversation for a minute. I saw how hurt mom was from it, an adult taken something from your child and it was stolen.

Auntie is ninety years old and still has the diamond ring. She reminds me of it most of the time we see one another. This is an illustration of what people do to other people kids, those in the church do more damage than those not in the church. They turn their eyes to many things. It's about self-ishness and gain. This event left a mark on me. I unearthed the damage of life-threatening patterns.

I passed this kind of behavior onto my children as if it were accept-able. I'm unsure what the future holds for me, yet I do know failure pushed me, to try harder, but also to try differently. It has forced me to grow up and overcome hardship by standing on my own two feet. Only then can I find happiness. The diligent student inside me says I should get an A for the effort.

I would have been bored in auntie's home. I did not feel like watching a western movie with her. Late nights I would watch western movies with auntie as we gobble down maple walnut ice cream or pistachio ice cream with short bread cookies. I grew up being the baby for a long time. I became a loaner. I did not get the chance to play with many young kids growing up. The only time I enjoyed myself was when I visit and stay the night over my mom's sister house. My cousin and I were close in age. We played together, wore the same Easter dress to church shoes and tights our moms bought from Robert Hall stores. We received the same easy bake oven and Temby Tumble dolls every year for Christmas. We eventually outgrew this. Our moms were close did everything together basically. They did not grow up poor like we did. Their dad was a kingpin drug dealer. He got his hustle on selling drugs, running a restaurant, a club and rental property. We had to attend church on Sundays while over.

It was the same routine all the time. I stayed the night on a Saturday came home on Sunday evening. Mom would always be working to care for her four children. My brothers would stay the night sometimes with their oldest son. They would work their food truck that sold food candy and beverages in Stowe Village a housing project. My brothers would help their cousin get the truck prepared for the road and work it sometimes. This was the life for us having fun as a kid.

I am not afraid to tell my story. I'm too strong and spiritual to fear either the known or the unknown.

In 1969, police raided my aunt and her husband's home in a prominent all-white suburb Not only did the Hartford and East Hartford police ransack the home, but also the feds, ravenously, the searched both of their home. After they diligently searched for heroin, they realized there may be at others houses.

These folks believed they could just do us any o'l way and do nothing about it because they carry firearms. Although at least they did not make a mess in the children's room, since there obviously would not be anything illicit in there. Those who came to support auntie was detained until after the raid, unexpectedly. There were narcotic detectives all over their home turning over couches, appliances, held mom, Joey my oldest brother, grandma, auntie, and her children. These officers grew furious when they did not locate the huge shipment.

One of the detectives shoved Joey who was only eleven years old. Mom lost it: She grabbed the narcs gun and all of whom witnessed this could not prevent anyone from assaulting a young kid. This woke everyone up who would have never thought this could be. Mother was angry at one person who was acting brolic shoving someone's child for no reason. They talked mom out of it before anything happened firing the gun into the floor before dropping it.

On a tip someone contacted the feds searched their other property. Someone knew something there they sent a trailer to pick an excavator to excavate the driveway pavement there. It was the big shipment of drugs valued at two million dollars.

The privilege of a lifetime is being who you are.

—Joseph Campbell

It's not everyday a worker at the police department is arrested. The police department issued a thousand-dollar cash bond which was paid, mother was home same day. Mom was released from her job. She did receive visits from her job the Hartford Police Department from a detective Bolling who came by to check on her as well. The police department detective was at fault. There was something both sides agreed upon charges were dismissed released from her job and life moved on. Mom was not pleased with this scenario, yet she was pleased to know she was not having no officer take advantage of her or disrespect her or her child in the presence of anyone. She did not wish for me to ever mention this ever again to anyone. I mentioned it sometimes in my lifetime, although

These kinds of events reflect the necessity of the Black Lives Matter movement and Civil Rights movement. As Black people, we often fail to recognize how the legacy of slavery affects us and everyone else. In the moment of tragedy, it can be especially difficult to connect how generational trauma impacts our personal trauma.

I know of many people out there willing to talk to federal agents. Some share everything, they know, and others lie. In every circumstance, the common denominator is fear. Police pressure individuals with the threat of prison unless they cooperate. And authorities readily accept the testimony of these individuals regardless of whether it is true.

My children's dad became an informant against me. He never once considered all of mine he possessed—a Range Rover, my retail military store, a couple homes including one on the marina, and more. He would eventually marry—I never married him since I knew from the beginning, he wasn't loyal. His wife is chronically ill and his stepson is a child molester. Both these people lived in the same house as my children while I sat in federal prison and made raising my kids incredibly difficult for me. He and the wife refused to allow me to co-parent.

Although both acted in conjunction, it was the wife who, as a Christian, did everything she could to keep the kid's dad and me away from each other. Profoundly insecure wife was not done playing house with him and our two kids. She knew he was not done with me. He indulged her. The spouse did not care to feel she was a rebound taking care a man and his young children. She felt the need to feel sorry for him because he had a newborn baby and a toddler. She hears so much about me she knew she had no other choice but to marry him. She wanted all this chaos. She went out her way to conceive being it was difficult for her. Guilt consumed him. For reasons I still do not fully understand, they even painted me badly to our children. He later apologized to me for his behavior. I asked why he did it? What was the real reason, or should I have insinuated what I already know? During my incarceration, I left him comfortable with two beautiful homes, a range rover, money, and love. His second wife he married while I was incarcerated.

She put my fifteen-year-old teenager out her house. Our daughter reminded her of me. When our kids were much younger, both did not want me to have my kids. They both received their very own karma. They both in and out of hospital not believing they would get their karma for their pathetic deeds they did, because they both were yet holding onto other drama and wanted to use me as the reason.

I filed petitions to see my kids for when I had visits and came to CT on furloughs. They both did not know why both would go out their way to belittle me with my kids. She did not know he became an informant against me. As far as her, she was bored and insecure about me. Who would do this as a Christian feel threatened to try to harbor a mother's young kids? Every time she seen me, she wanted to call the police.

It became a game he played with her to keep her happy because he resided in her home, they got together without his name on the deed or loan, so he was homeless and did not know it being married to her.

At the federal prison I was at, there was open door policy whereas we as inmates could always go to the warden and the associate warden office anytime, their offices were open. I get approached by the associate warden one day, an African American woman. She was polite every bit of someone who had my side in this matter, told me she received a letter or call, requesting I do not send any correspondence to her house.

In the essence of it she was ask was the kids her and Buno kids she said no. She asks was the kids my birth kids she said yes. She did know I not long ago gave birth to a baby while in prison, so she knew something about me reading my presentence investigative report. The associate warden told Fe-Fe she cannot ask me not to send correspondence to her residence being my kids are residing there, I have every right too.

I left my kids with their father not her. She decided to marry the kids' father for whatever known reason to help him. The associate warden and I both laughed at her pathetically. I than begin to send more letters to the kids and Buno just because she is now insecure.

She would now have to get a court order and that is not going to happen. This woman did not know me, she had my appliances in her home and some furniture we shared together. I could not believe she would even want my things never mind the man.

I must admit it was hard being incarcerated for five years and have a man you have two kids by turn his back on you with your kids, take your possessions get married rollover and become an informant. All of this because he was homeless someone who claim to be a hustler. She enjoyed every bit of it and yet still miserable with him. It's all about me I am that powerful to them. A wave of peace washed over me. I praised God for because I were able to see clearly. He will get his karma as well as her.

The Holy Spirit showed me him being married prior we were dating him so marrying her why should it bother me now because he's married again. I begin to accept we just wasn't for one another. I needed my babies in my life. In retrospect Buno did not know how to be self-sufficient or independent without being codependent.

Thankfully, his habits did not shackle my emotions anymore. Relationships such as this are put together superficially. Really caring about what society has to say than just leaving the relationship. He must stick around to get his share. What he did not know he did not have to stick around for his share. All he had to do is see a lawyer and get his share.

She does not know me but always gave negative remarks about me because I'm a felon and so is he. I refused him in marriage three times. There was something that kept me afraid of the knowing. And he did not have anything to bring to the table as a woman besides babies. I had young kids from ex-husband.

They both received their karma, and I am cool. I'm not sick with anything praise God.

It is cathartic to believe peoples' insecurities and sicknesses are what sabotage our relationships. In my piety, I recognized my kids' father had yet to fully mature. He later had another child with his second wife, and that is okay—if he does not have another with me was her issue, nothing ever speculated with what I know of this woman.

God honors marriage. Who buys a home and does not allow the spouse to add their name on the deed when both have income? It was always her home, but my daughter had to leave it at age fifteen. Buno's wife put her out, and I had to step in after substantial drama. She never liked my daughter, and she made her feel unloved and unwanted from the exposure to trauma. Wherever I saw them again, I promised to punch the caddy chick in her face for pretending to love my daughter. She withheld any compassion for my daughter not because of her character, but purely because I was her mother. Meanwhile, she treats his other daughters with love because they have different mothers. She doesn't feel threatened by any of them.

You become what you think about.

—Earl Nightingale

Things do not change; we change.

—Henry David Thoreau

I could've done anything I ever wanted to do and more. With so many felonies on my record, I now have no other choice than to work for myself and create my own stream of income. Good faith from others is all I ever wanted, and today, with all my strength, I internalize it.

My greatest discovery was that I hold the key to my freedom. The key is my spirit. As you continue to read my story, I would like to offer you encouragement. This is my story as I see and remember it. It has nothing to do with anybody else or how they see it. I hope you will read my story with the awareness that we all must see what others see in order to grow. My goal is to depict the lessons we must master through the experiences we encounter.

In my journey, I have practiced daily spiritual exercises. As a result, I have learned to let go and to stop resisting or fighting. I must deliver my everyday life into the hands of God, my personal redeemer. I would like for you to know how I found peace in my broken life. One powerful stress management tool I use is meditation.

To heal, one must understand no one is immune to life's challenges. I will share with you that I have learned about the power of family patterns and the permanent scars they leave in one's life. The presence and the power of these patterns live in our blood, solidify our spiritual foundation, and anoint our relationship with God. As the scriptures say, we as daughters will experience what God says we will experience.

Father will be divided against son and son against father, mother against daughter and daughter against mother, and mother-in-law against daughter-in-law and daughter-in-law against mother-in-law.

—Luke 12:53 (NKJV)

For too long, I did not understand what I could have in the spirit. Discovery consists in seeing what everyone else has seen and thinking what no one else has thought.

—Albert Szent-Gyorgy

Suspicious, curious, and concerned as a child, I asked both parents questions, but always received lies. This is the case even with respectful, great parents where children begin to learn to lie because their parents told them lies. To learn to live with it and take it to their grave harms our psyche and our spirit.

Of the many things I have learned in my life, I know of nothing else that had as much impact as realizing the only One I can depend on is God. Without any doubt, I know He is the only One who has turned me around, pushed me down, pushed me back, pushed me forward, moved me along, taught me what I needed to know, and reminded me of what I already knew. At just the right time, in his perfect way, God will do the same in you, through you, and for you.

Now, I have life because I look to my Creator for all things. I have learned to conserve my strength for what counts, what I can change, and what I can control. Each day, I face new challenges. I spend quality time with my children and grandchildren.

Blind spots obscured my vision for years, until I discovered a center and source for my life. God is faithful and just to forgive me. I will not allow for life to leave me without making a positive impact here on Earth. Many times, I served as judge, jury, and prosecutor. I gave myself a life sentence of mourning and regret. Now, I live with conviction. I no longer spend my life in the graveyard of guilt and shame with the corpse of my past.

I was born in sin, shaped in iniquity, then raised in the church. As a grown adult, I took the responsibility of attending church on my own. I realized that I am not the woman I thought I was. I had to learn who I am. My gift is not for me, but for everyone.

My soul triumphed as sifting through. My life a surge of energy straightened with pride. The truth I have known all my life is I had the potential to be an Ivy League student. But part of me was afraid of shining so brightly. When I was older and started getting arrested, I felt contriteness. If only there were someone to tell me, *Girl, you are going to do it. You are going to graduate with honors. You are going to be a great attorney or psychologist.* I have known for years I needed to share my life story. I began other books that, to my sorrow, I never completed. I worried about the repercussions of exposing those who have done me wrong.

You do not get away with sin—you pay for it. I thank God, He took me to my lowest point, for I found Jesus there. I was on the ground, and I did not die. *Thank God!* There are folks who know I matter. They know God's hands are on me. They navigate through our frustration just to see how I do it. These are those who are not invited, yet they try to come along. You must watch these types of people. It is hard to please everyone. Some people act as if they aren't broken when they are; some smile as if they're happy when they're not; some act as if they're happily married when they're not.

Hypocrite simply means *actor*—it's not a bad word. It is different when you're trying to live a victorious life while going through an ordeal. People cannot live everything they preach—no one can. Otherwise, Jesus would not have had to die. He would have been a hypocrite to act like you aren't doing anything wrong. God will not send you to hell for speaking your truth. Church is the only place you could do what you want to do act out speak out and not get fired for it. This does not even happen in the White House. They are not going to pay your mortgage, nor give you a loan, so you have nothing to lose except maybe have to find yourself a new church.

A hidden connection is stronger than an obvious one.

—Heraclitus of Ephesus

Who I am has been shaped by my life experiences, most of which were beyond my control? God molded me through my family, challenges, every pleasant and painful event, every death, my marriages, my relationships, my work, my education, and my spiritual experience. He used all these to prepare me for what He called me to do. My ministry now is to help those who experience the same thing I did but are too ashamed to admit it. God wants my past to inform my mission.

I have no problem telling others the truth. In all my trials and blessings, God's grace has assisted me. My purpose and my life are far more meaningful than my own material fulfillment. I didn't understand this principle until now. Since I was convicted of crimes repeatedly, my quest for money cost me my life. I had no idea where my life was going. I now know I will turn tragedies into strategies.

Married

What a wonderful thought it is that some of the best days of our lives haven't even happened yet.

—Anne Frank

EVERYTHING I EVER YEARNED FOR was related to my children, my husband, and myself. When our children were young, we divorced, yet it was all about me. Things I did for myself did not include my Creator at all. Everything I did was for the wrong reason I subconsciously knew the truth, but I didn't do what I thought I believed I could do. I did not understand why. I was busy without a purpose and no center. My Creator desired all of me and I knew it. I was married and profoundly unhappy. It may have looked as if I was happy, but truly, I was miserable.

Clem, my ex-husband, was a good man, and since he was in the building trade, we had a good life. Trust permeated our marriage. He gave me everything I desired. Still, he struggled with his own issues. A hole existed inside him. He was still hurting from losing his father when he was eighteen. When we started a family, he didn't know how to be a father. He insisted on a particular martial agreement I accepted, even though I had my own income as well.

Clem put me on a pedestal. However, he also combated addiction. When he didn't get what he wanted from me, he'd tried to tear me down. At an early age, I was tired of plodding around the mulberry bush with him. His addiction kept me committing crimes when I did not want to in order to support my family. I grew sick and exhausted with him as he played the *I'm-going-to-leave-you* game. He being insecure about my youth wanted to keep me stuck holding onto him afraid I would leave him. I looked at him as a father figure. We did a lot of interesting things together and communicated the things we were both embarrassed to admit. That was good for our relationship. I do not believe he was accepting or ready for me to acknowledge he thirteen years older than me. I am grown, matured, and respectful to accepting those things I cannot change. I will not threaten a man in a relationship when it will not work. I could not see myself being unhappy yet young and had a life ahead of me, with four young children or not.

As for me I see it a waste of time to maintain a partnership where only one person has their desires met. Both people often know they will never attain their fairy tale vision with each other, yet they prefer to hold on to *nothing*!

Resolved, I decided I would be all right with my kids without him. Clem had taken me for granted. We had our own home, two businesses, his building trade as a sprinkler fitter, and my income. When we divorced, I received our marital home, the kids, child support, half of one of his pensions, parts of his Social Security as arrearage of child support. I had my Range Rover I purchased with my own cash. This was my lifestyle before him, with him, and after him. My second Range Rover came with my second home on the marina after my divorce. I received a lump sum from him. Oh, was Clem furious! He wanted me to flounder financially. Some man, huh? I refused to do badly just because he was unhappy with himself.

The agency gave us a cease-and-desist order to close the telemarketing business. One of the businesses I sold to Woody, who was a known hustler later-turned federal informant. Woody informed the Feds against Clem and I. Woody earned a lot of income from the business he purchased, not as much as I did.

When I was married, I earned a decent income with my employer before I ever started working for myself. Later, in 1992, my telemarketing companies brought my annual income to a little over a hundred thousand dollars. Clem decided to take a break and enjoy time with our kids. It seemed as though all the money we had come from my hard work. He was just in the way.

My spirituality soared high during this time in my life, though I was not sure if it was because I was married or because of my renewed sense of God's presence. Although I love God, I didn't know Him like I do today. When I sinned, I repented. Eventually, my conscience evaporated, and I no longer seemed to care. For fourteen years, I once again habitually committed crimes with pleasure. These patterns controlled me, and I did not understand why. That it kept happening scared me.

We both spent long hours with infertility physicians to try to conceive. I took Clomid and pergonal injections for three years. On one occasion, the doctor saw two eggs, which would have been twins, and asked if I would like to have them fertilized. I had been told it would be risky to carry the babies, and I wasn't up for it at all. Mother even wanted to be a surrogate for us.

I went ahead and had other procedures done to see what had prevented my pregnancy. Apparently, I had a couple of cysts; however, they were not blocking anything and were non-cancerous. The doctor performed artificial insemination on me with Clem, and it worked the first try. Both Clem and I were thrilled.

Two OB/GYN physicians cared for me and my unborn baby Andrew, who was my second child. I came across a story in the Bible about a woman who went through the same thing. She wanted a baby so badly she promised she would give her child back to God in holiness and train him to serve the Lord. However, I did not follow this path. I spoke to God in prayer about Andrew.

Years later, my son was held in a Maryland prison on charges of first-degree murder, second-degree murder, involuntary manslaughter, and possession of a firearm. I took leadership on building his defense. If nothing else, I had to be there for my child, and it felt good. I Googled and interviewed attorneys there in the Maryland area who had experience winning murder trials. I used specific keywords: *federal prosecutor experience, trial experience, state court prosecutor experience,* and *photos.* As I searched, visions of my dreams for a big family flashed before me. Only by diligently bothering God for babies did I have my children. I remember thinking, *if anything ever happened, what would I do to protect my kids?* I said, *do all a mother should do.* And that is what I did.

Andrew, meanwhile, was impatient. He wanted another lawyer because he thought his attorney moved too slowly. *That is crazy,* I thought. I'd gone through all the work of interviewing, driving to Baltimore to meet with the attorney, and sending payments. I had also been visiting Andrew, adding money to commissary and to his phone calls, buying him books, and getting him anything he wanted for the holidays and for his girlfriend. Only a mother would have done this much.

I remember before this happened, a small, still voice said to me, *what if one of your children got him- or herself in serious trouble—like murder? How would you react?* The cost of a lawyer is more than some people's yearly income, and you pay for what you get. It costs even more for an attorney to go to trial, and most want their funds upfront. I spoke on the phone with Andrew three or four times a day. I knew he was going through something more than anyone who has never been to prison can fathom. This experience reminded him to look diligently to God for all things. I knew he was angry with God because I could not be with him or his siblings when I was in prison. I always had to stop him before he said something foolish out of rage.

At trial, a jury found him not guilty on all charges except for a possession of a firearm. Praise God! After the verdict was read, I fell to the floor, pressed my forehead to the ground, and thanked God for His grace and mercy called on Jesus. One of the sheriffs, as he helped me up with jurors looking on, told me I could not do this had to get up. I looked upon this sheriff as man you do not understand God and His presence. Out of consideration to the victim's family, the judge sentenced Andrew to three years to for the possession of firearm charge. Hallelujah to Jesus!

I taught Andrew how to use yoga and meditate to access his third eye. Andrew did well for himself prior to his arrest for the murder in Baltimore. He earned a decent income working at the union. I look at this Baltimore incident as a bump in the road. Now it's over, thank God. I remember the expression of relief on Andrew's face after he saw me in the courtroom. *The devil*, I thought, *is after our children and our household*. When it comes to our loved ones and us, we must fight the devil at all costs and not let him win at anything. I knew Andrew needed me there. His father was seventy-one and unable to travel much, although he did attend a few court hearings. Still, his prayers and soul were there for Andrew. We went to other court appearances prior to the trial. Since he was out of state, participating in his appearances could be challenging, especially for his friends and siblings who have families of their own. I was the one who went the most. I had to be there for my child, and I thanked God I could be.

It was during the time I had a retail millinery unisex store in the shopping center that I found myself in a relationship with Buno, who, as I mentioned earlier in my story, was not in love with his wife. A known drug dealer, Buno was the kind of person I said I would never get myself involved with growing up and I did.. But foolishly, I thought I needed a partner whose income matched mine. Even though my net worth was far greater than his, I decided this was something I wanted to do and not make excuses for myself. I was thirty-five with over four-hundred thousand in assets, alone with my children. I did not know what else to do. There were no females in my era who had what I had at my age in the hood or as a hustler. As a young girl, I had seen my aunt's husband made babies on her with other women, so I guess Buno doing the same did not seem unusual to me.

After thirty days, the man I found myself involved with left his significant other and asked me to marry him. The situation bothered me, but

I could not place my finger on why. I know I'm valuable, smart, attractive, and hilarious. He was six years younger than me. He knew my income was greater. I was a mother figure to him since he was a momma's boy was where the attraction started, I believe. His first wife saw I wasn't going anywhere. I was not pressured into being with him. I learned to love him. I was bored with my husband. He played with his ex before me and thought I was blindsided. At the same time. My young children always kept me busy.

I started dating him after his marriage crumbled. He had married young only because she was pregnant. The first wife, Barbara, had him served with separation papers at the club he hung out at thought it would get to him, being she had been upset about the situation very badly. The same day Buno called me to ask me to start his divorce papers. I set to work quickly because this is something he wanted. I worked out of the home office I have had for many years as a entrepreneur.

Sometimes when a person really wants to end a relationship, that desire pushes them to do the thing they are most afraid to do. In Buno's case I thought he most feared his wife but that was not the case at all. He so badly wanted out the marriage. He was always in other relationships but felt somewhat compelled the years he was there because of the two daughter they have together. He had a total of five children then. One, already an adult, he had by a Caucasian woman. Everyone knew and accepted the situation for what it was, except his wife, to whom he continued to lie too. He was sad news always lied about anything.

Real women do not play any games, unless remaining in the partnership is a choice and they have a game plan. He stated the only reason he married Barbara was because she was p regnant. He had little money and his mother felt it was the right thing to do. Why not? Still, marrying her was not what he wanted to do. He could not see her with him all his life tired of fighting with her about other women. He did not see her as a total turn on.

Barbara was a jealous person who could not believe her spouse divorced her for an older woman. I thought, just let it go! Because he left her, this chick contacted the Assistant United States Attorney's Office and gave them information she fabricated regarding us. I begged him twice to go back to her due to the lies she talked about me. I managed things the way I knew how when miserable females become vindictive. His wife's sister-in-law, Mamie, could tell you I made both their lives uncomfortable. They did not know what I could do.

When Buno moved out, she and her mother tried to block him with their vehicles; they would not let him leave with his personal possessions. He let Barbara have the family home being she did not have anywhere to take kids. She is unable to pay the mortgage without him there. She soon moved somewhere cheaper than their mortgage. She let it lapse into foreclosure.

Buno's decision to leave her had little to do with me. He was unhappy with her and decided, regardless of the financial situation or the kids, he had to leave. Still, when it came to me, she always complained. She told me I was a homewrecker. Twice I called her to apologize and said he should return to his family. He did not want to, although, they continued to coparent. He sat behind my office door listening to my conversation with us talking on the telephone to her. Yet, he stayed.

He was a nice guy and a great provider, but I knew the relationship would not last. I live by principles, morals, and values, yet a force pulled me to do something I did not want to. I talked to God about the relationship. After three years, I knew it wasn't for me, so I ended it. Her lies in the aftermath did not really concern me. I was emotionally and financially established.

Buno was a drug dealer and had assets. He helped Barbara's mother buy her first home in the hood. She depended on his income for her entire family.

I do not know what it is with women who waste their precious time on a man who no longer wants a relationship with them. Their desperation comes from deep-rooted issues, often because their fathers abandoned them. Even if, as grown women, they are employed and financially independent, they fear loss. The man who cheats on his wife struggles with insecurity and sexual issues. However, the women act like I'm the problem when in fact their problem lies with their man.

Nobody can hurt me without my permission.

—Mahatma Gandhi

A jury of twelve eventually convicted me. I was sentenced to six years. I refused to accept the offer made. I was not guilty of the crimes in my business. My husband Clem was the owner, whereas I served solely as an elected officer.

Yet another accusation led to a mistrial, and a hung jury later found me solely guilty. There were always two prosecutors in the trials. Mrs. Otta the AUS Attorney who husband indicted on tax evasion her son indicted on drug sales which she implemented a hundred feet away from a school. Her very son was trapped. Meanwhile, my lawyer and her spouse attended baseball games with their grandkids in limos. Another one of the AUS Attorneys had a Napoleon Complex. Mr. Bailey was short with light skin and glasses. An undersized, overconfident, bourgeois man, Mr. Bailey wanted to keep me always scared of him and that did not ever happen.

Our legal team won every round of the trial. Ms. Otta and I would smile tightly at each other from across the courtroom when she scored or when Mack, my attorney, would score.

Then, something happened. The government suddenly did everything in their power to win their case against me. Although Clem and I worked as a team, the government wanted only me.

Aloud Clem ask the court for mercy just send him to prison in the case. He defended me.

This way, I could stay at home to care for our young children and maintain our assets.

The government was upset I earned $2.2 million dollars within eighteen months. I worked for a company, and once I learned every aspect of the business, I felt the need to start my own. I knew the rules about former felons owning companies could be legally challenging. Before I worked for myself, I had consulted with Mr. Jeremy, a corporate prestige lawyer and a prosecutor in state court for a decade. Since the rules are a gray area, he gave me permission to go ahead. He later testified in the case.

The government painted a picture of me as a cagey and witty person. They strung together evidence from their informant Woody. Mack, a sharp-witted man, approached his case from the jurors' standpoint. He and his family practiced in their home before dinner. The government, meanwhile, chose a young Portuguese gangster prosecutor and another whose fiancé was a white-collar high-profile attorney. The latter advised the prosecution to prejudice the jurors with my company income, spouse's income, and my own income. Never mine setting the trial up with entering exhibits of a informant who bought one of my businesses who later turned rat.

The government had no pity in my case. At the time, I was expecting a baby. They did not care. I had not been arrested in nineteen years. Still, they did not care. The government then decided to play dirty since I was in a new relationship with Buno. A known drug dealer introduced me to one of his business partners, who was also an informant in my case and others—Mr. Miller, an African. If Miller was getting paid, he did not fear what he faced. As well as not been arrested for his crimes. This is usually how it goes. Mack said Buno had also become an informant against me.

And I were sleeping with the enemy," he told me. I was shocked.

I could never fathom why Buno constantly asked to marry me. Then the government would not be able to use him if we were married. Well, it is possible but difficult. Anyway, they allowed him to speak against me during my grand jury formal accusation, and to avoid being indicted himself, he lied to the grand jury with the assistance of the Assistant US Attorney. He and I were both made money, though I am not certain if they knew how much. The government felt Buno's testimony in my grand jury formal accusation was enough to convict me and prejudice the jury, and that is exactly how it happened. From the outside looking in. I got a full view of how the jurors viewed cases. Young jurors especially are much easier to work with. Older people have the tendency to believe someone in a white shirt or participates in the law. This is a game of manipulation; the government seeks a win no matter how. All the income they claimed I had was because I was a wife with lavish things.

Woody was afraid of the Feds. Although Woody were arrested multiple times seen as a career criminal was serving an eight-year sentence was about to end. He was leaving the jail on work release to work for me. He did what he wanted in out of jail. Woody did not ever have a case with the feds. He was afraid of them as many folks who are afraid of them. Look at Trump friends most of them did not tell on Trump. They did not have too. They created their own involvement being greedy. They had as much earnings as Trump. He did not wish to leave his girlfriends or his main lady on the outside alone again. Clem and I did not know why, suddenly, Woody no longer came to our residence. He stopped by every day when he worked for us. Even when he purchased his own business, he would still visit frequently. We were skeptical until we received a call from our corporate attorney asking us to come to his office. He said he needed to inform us of a message from U.S. Attorney John Durham. We were to no longer communicate with Woody because he was now cooperating with the Feds against us.

Corruption is rampant in the judicial system. In a more recent example, former AG Bill Barr's employee did an investigation on corruption with Ukraine on the question of interference in the 2016 election. Bill Barr then used his power to divert media attention, stating he did not find any evidence. All along, he knew Russia sabotaged the 2016 election in favor of Trump.

In my first trial with the government, both AUS Attorneys were fired because of their conduct. They submitted nonevidence to the jury to convict me when they were losing. The tension in the case arose when my best friend at the time, Charlotte, decided to take part of my business to her apartment. There, away from oversight, she robbed the customers. When they caught her, she blamed Clem and me. She swindled customers out of thousands of dollars, but instead of returning to prison, Charlotte became an informant for the Feds. The government also gave Charlotte a job with social security for about fifteen years. She did wrong on her own something she did not feel would happen knowingly protecting herself.

Anyway, I could not believe someone who had been in the game as a hustler as long as Woody would become an informant (I was shocked about Charlotte, too). Woody felt nothing when we saw him in passing; his face remained stoic and unaffected. He would not return to prison now, and this comforted him. The Feds had his back. On the drawing board in one of the trials, Mack showed the court that the government had offered Woody a 501K Snitch Rule.

"Is this," Mack asked Woody, "what the government presented to you for your assistance?"

"Yes," came the reply.

The next two assistant state's attorneys furiously pursued my conviction in whatever way they could, and they did. I will never forget Ms. Peck and Mr. Genco. They went to extremes to win. Even with their tactics, they won only after trying three times over six years. I was given seventy-two months in Danbury Federal Prison. Upon my incarceration, I was designated to Carlswell Texas Medical because I was eight months pregnant. While at Danbury, I put papers in for a transfer to go—Alderson Federal Prison Country Club.

Prison there was different. We resided in cottages and had keys to our doors. Family day came once every year, with a carnival on the camp-grounds, family stay house for visitors, or your family would pay and stay at any hotel or motel in the area. My family stayed at a Marriot when I did a seventy-two-hour furlough. We ate at the Marriot and many restaurants; we swam in the Jacuzzi and watched movies with the kids. After the furlough went smoothly, I asked for a seven-day furlough. Five- or seven-day leaves were available, although no one I knew were granted the seven days because it was easier to ask for five days granted seven. Then everyone who were eligible for a furlough was putting their papers in for seven days. I put my papers in, and they were approved by Scibana, the warden outstanding stupendous man. That was a blessing. The two-assistant state attorneys, meanwhile, held a party to celebrate their new conviction.

We don't see things as they are, we see them as we are.

—Anais Nin

You gain strength, courage and confidence by every experience in which you really stop and look fear in the face ... You must do the thing which you think you cannot do.

—Eleanor Roosevelt

I first gave my life to Christ at twelve years old. I grew up in a Pentecostal church, where praising God was all, we did. We shook tambourines, banged on drums, sang in choir, and listened to sermons.

We got our *shout on* praising God. I wanted to accept Christ as my Lord and Savior just as my mother and grandmother did. They were spiritual, and I wanted to emulate their lives. I attended Sunday church service, Bible study, and Wednesday night prayer service with my mother and family.

My dad was not a churchgoer at all, but when I was a child, all four kids went to church. After I got married, my husband sometimes went too, but mostly just the kids and I went.

I was in the family choir at age six. Our choir cut a 45rpm called "Gospel Lights." My uncle was the choir director. Although as an adult I am not a singer, I wish I still sang in the family choir. I really do enjoy gospel music.

What is more, I learned through life, teaching is vital to the church. I received Christ when I was twenty-four years old, but I fell in and out of sin. I did whatever I wanted, only to immediately repent. Ignorant spiritual people follow this pattern. They don't know what they're doing, and in repeating their mistakes, they test a might, jealous God who create everything for His purpose. I am created as a special object of God's love. God made me for a reason, and my life has profound meaning. I discovered this when I made God the reference point in my life. I now know I am uniquely created for what I always thought of myself, no doubt. I struggled with this for a long time. I finally have the strength to accept the things I could not change. The scriptures came alive in my pain. They thrived in my trauma, which itself came alive while I was in prison. There were suicides, the beating of inmates by correctional officers, and many of the inmates and staff had wicked spiritual demons.

When things are bad, you must tolerate them. There are some situations may strike you as nonsense, yet this is life. When negativity persist, your endurance increases. Your greatest fears sometimes become reality. I was powerless and afraid, and I had to put all my faith in God through prayer. I also had to own my faults. My heart no longer raced, and my terrible thoughts ceased. I had to learn balance – to be the woman I imagined myself as when I was a child. I learned to strive instead of struggle. In many bad moments, I'm sure you've faced these challenges. Today, I know what it is to live. When trouble persists long enough, one learns to accept what we cannot alter. I am powerless, and what I choose to do now does not resemble what I use to do. My temptations were of materialism, convenience, and comfort. As I reflect on my situation in and out of prison, I see those temptations were a lie told by Satan.

I am free, no matter what rules surround me. If I find them tolerable, I tolerate them: if I find them to   obnoxious, I break them. I am free because I know that I alone am morally responsible for everything I do

—Robert A. Heinlein

What we remember from childhood we remember forever—
permanent ghosts, stamped, inked, imprinted, eternally seen.

—Cynthia Ozick

The story written by my faults is one I inherited from my father. He gave me his eyes, nose, and ears—as well as his addiction to a life of corruption. Habits are hard to break. Yet, for fourteen to nineteen years, I avoided state prison before I did federal time. I became loyal to my family's dysfunctional patterns. Now, I see I was experiencing self-abuse and denial.

This is the story of how I learned to tell the truth about myself. A broken little girl becomes a broken woman who creates a broken life because she needs broken people to support the safe fiction, she has created. These were not bad people. However, they were teachers of the highest order because they drove me straight into the arms of God.

This is the fabric from which I am cut. At an incredibly early age, I told myself I wanted to be like my dad without knowing how corrupt my father's life really was. When I was five or six years old, I remember playing in my parents' room with my mother's pearls. There, I discovered an article from the *Hartford Courant* in her jewelry box. I knew the article meant something—I was in the reading group, which was the top reading group in my class—and I could understand the importance of the words, though I did not fully comprehend them. My dad was one of the greatest hustlers in his field, and I thought the same about myself. That is my insanity. This is what kept me hustling and getting myself into trouble with the law.

There were things no one taught me—things that would have changed the way I saw myself and lived my life. My mom did not teach me about womanhood or parenthood, love or sex, or vision or purpose. I did learn the basics—how to keep my body and home clean. I learned to make the best of what I had and dampen my ambitions. I learned how to avoid, ignore, or dismiss the truth. As my story progressed, I created the exact negative scenarios in my life my dad modeled for me.

I was not taught to make choices; I was not taught to be responsible for myself; I wasn't taught to receive or give love, nor was I shown how to distinguish between those who truly loved me and those who only claimed to love me. In the absence of guidance, I made up my own sense of others and myself. It was a relief when I learned the truth. I realized I could change the insanity.

My mother never talked to me about anything I would face as a woman. Although, when I was five, she taught me not to allow a man to touch me between my legs, she did not give me any other guidance. My mother remained my only source of wisdom since my dad was in prison twice during my life. My mother, however, worked eighty hours a week. She did not have time to spend with me. Sometimes, we would go out to dinner at a restaurant during the week, and we attended church together.

She did not give me instructions on my mind or my heart. I was not taught anything about how to interact with a man other than what I witnessed from my mother and other family members, who were dysfunctional. I learned the truth only when I was much older. Things I believed were good, honestly, were not. My grandparents slept in separate beds. My grandmother took all my grandfather's hard-earned money and bought lavish things. She traded in her car every two years, bought furs, traveled on a regular basis, bought expensive clothing, and paid the mortgage for an expensive house. She also did not work other than care for foster children and babysit.

My mother and my father, similarly imperfect, were divorced after eighteen years of marriage. Her second husband was from Jamaica, and she sponsored him. My little brother Maurice came from this marriage, at which point they had been married thirty-four years. She needed someone other than my father. She was too young not to be in a relationship.

My mother did not sleep around nor have many men in her life. She and my grandmother both ruled their men and gathered the money. My mother always said she was in love with my father and would get back with him. In the end, she did. They spent their last ten years together before departing this earth.

It doesn't matter who my father was; it matters who I remembered he was.

—Anne Sexton

Neglect devastates parents and children alike. When a person responsible for a child's best interest fails to safeguard the child's emotional and physical well-being, it is a passive form of abuse. Whether it results from poverty, carelessness, or a chaotic homelife, child neglect tends to be more common and more chronic than violence. Often, neglect is subtle because there appears to be logical explanations for the caregiver's behavior, and so the abuse goes unrecognized. If the parent does not intend to harm the child, those who do notice are hesitant to interfere.

My parents only knew what they were taught to do when it came to raising their kids. I always knew they did their best even when we were adults. However, they consistently and persistently ignored my need for nurturing, encouragement, education, and protection.

The wounds inflicted on children by adults does more than just devastate; it saps the strength and vitality of a young person's heart and mind. Those wounds weaken her will to live and grow and distort and deplete her God-given right to explore possibilities and experience a life of divinity. Children of unsupportive parents feel inadequate, ineffective, and victimized as they move through adolescence and into adulthood.

The Feds and Informants

WHEN YOU DO NOT KNOW who you are, chances are you don't know what you want. When you do not know what you want, there's no chance you will get it.

My dad went down in history in a court case known as *J. Wilson vs. State of Connecticut*. He won a precedent in the Supreme Court while incarcerated in the 1960s. Well-regarded in prison, my dad had things in his cell other inmates did not. I met a guard who worked at the men's prison for twenty-five years and knew my dad. I cleaned their offices at the women's facility, where the guard then worked. A Christian, he told me my dad was a bigwig in prison and a good guy, which I knew.

I have always taken pride in my parents. They were both great; they were not drug addicts, my mother was not forced into prostitution, and they didn't fight—or if so, they never did it around the kids. They were just working-class people who cared for their children in a productive home. When I was an adult, my mother told me my dad received so much prison time because the authorities suspected him of criminal activity they could not prove. Since he was affiliated with organized crime, he may even have been involved in murders. I do not know. He was not the average street hustler. We both came from the same dna.

My story resembles my dad's. I challenged the Feds in three trials, and I only lost the third trial. The assistant attorneys prejudiced the jurors with Clem and my personal income. I won notoriety when attorneys Ms. Otta and Mr. Bailey were both terminated from their positions as an outcome of their attempts to falsely convict me. This was not printed by any reporters or in any media. And we did not get any relief from it other than a new trial because Ms. Otta and Mr. Bailey entered exhibits, they should not have to prejudice the juror to believe a lie. People without money or influence seem to quickly fall victim to these tactics, whereas those with money seldom receive prison time.

I once greatly respected my friend Charlotte. I meet her in prison in 1984, a roommate, heroin addict, became a informant to the feds. The day Charlotte became one she tried using the Lord a reason she did what she did. However, she had committed many crimes using my business while at her residence. The feds gave her a job in the Social Security office thanked her for her cooperation. They used her for fifteen years, she ends up losing her job. She later turned back to her former addiction – drugs and alcohol. I never once did her any wrong nor ask her to commit any crimes, all she did she did on her own for herself and told lies on me to protect herself.

Both my former friend's and associates, Charlotte and Woody, acted out of corruption. They stole from customers failed to send out their products. When employees were calling to resell customers products, we heard stories this person received their money and did not send them anything. The government received a whiff of this and did nothing because she's now a informant against Clem and me. It was in my heart to have harm done to Charlotte, but the feds were watching me. They protect their informant's, if they testify and win their case. I noticed cars with tinted windows pulled away as soon as I backed my car of my garage. I was livid and tired of the feds. The feds would go to court seeking a superseding indictment seeking to add more than do not meet the offense to win a conviction. We know how they do us add all types of charges to the arrest and having a difficult time charging Donald J. Trump who constantly commits felonies persistently and no one would like to indict him but have this superseding long investigation bs.

Charlotte was not so good on the phone to solicit customers. She felt as though because she receives a decent paycheck, she was doing the thing. I'm starting out with a new company. She's like any other broke disadvantage person who will take advantage of anyone who has money. I had the money.

A successful businesswoman who worked for herself and helped others something some do not do unless their forced to do it. I made myself a promise I would not permit my children to experience what I did. I was determined to give my children whatever they needed to feel wanted, welcomed, and loved. If they had educational opportunities, I thought they would avoid trouble. Over the decades, while engaged in my own life, I forgot my children were also living their lives. They begin to see what I saw, Unacceptable, I thought. I was unequipped to do anything about it. I did what I knew to do but turned away my head, eyes, and ears. But then I had to come to grips and accept my flaws. We come to a place in life we are not who we intended to be in life. My children's souls have assignments just like mine.

Growing up, I knew we were poor but not poe! I adapted to my environment with or without labels. I have learned what to accept and what to except in response to what I see, hear, or am taught. As I aged, I' am learning to be myself. For a long time, I knew neither who I was not who I should be.

Relationships

All sorrows can be borne if you put them into a story or tell a story about them.

—Karen Blixen

SPIRITUALITY IS CRUCIAL TO FULL recovery from any psychological condition. To discover and ultimately liberate one's true self—our inner child—we need spirituality. No matter how distant she may seem, we each have an inner child who is energetic and alive. Our true self lies in her. If your inner child is improperly nourished or denied freedom, a false self emerges.

The accumulation of emotional and mental traumas can lead to anxiety, unhappiness, fear, and a sense of emptiness. When we form codependent relationships, we deny our inner child—a common habit among children and adults who grew up in troubled families affected by mental illness or neglect.

We must recognize certain principles to discover who we really are, and in so doing, we may recover from or diminish our pain, suffering, and confusion. To practice these principles takes effort, time, and discipline. For so many years, I carried the scar of my rape into relationships and marriage. I could not put the pieces together until I reflected on my life. My perspective now enables me to connect the links and transform dysfunctional relationships into healthier ones—with children, siblings, grandchildren, and others. By nurturing myself, I love myself.

The rape will no longer hover over my life; it's dead, and I do not have room for it. Today, I have the self-esteem, power, and confidence to easily move forward. I thank God, He embraced me in His unconditional love.

Happy or not, my relationship stories are a part of me. What kept me with someone was my stupidity. I did not want to be alone, nor did I have many options for men. In the beginning, I dated Pop, whom I liked a lot; however, his behavior made me uncomfortable. And, although I was independently minded, I was afraid to confront him. When I tried to get him to talk about our relationship, he got angry, and his behavior grew crueler and more manipulative. Early in our dating, I wanted to write him off. But the worse about how he treated me, the more dependent on him I became. This was the source of my unhappiness. No matter my intelligence, I became increasingly desperate to save it. We all try to float a sinking ship.

I later spiraled in shame, which, at that point, was a familiar pattern. Pop was not a real man. In retrospect, I only wish I walked away sooner. Instead, I continued to see him even after he moved out. I saw him even when I knew he was dating other women, although he denied it. I grew more upset at the person I had become than I was when I was about to lose him.

Every time I thought of my own behavior—how it weakened me and made many excuses I had made—I cringed. I did not feel like me. And yet, I was. Just remember—wanting to know where you stand in a relationship does not make one crazy or clingy. It just means you want to know if you should stop collecting names and numbers when you go out.

If your relationship is complicated and you are uncertain about your feelings, he or she is not the one! Romance was a game Pop played the women he dated as if he were a young boy. He sent them mixed signals so they would act crazy over him. He behaved in hurtful ways yet apologized for his conduct. The mixed signals should have warned me I needed to do something productive rather than wait around for this clown. What guy gets mad about discussing your relationship?

He wanted to avoid discomfort, so he did not break up with me; instead, he only grew more conflicted than he used to be. I became afraid to complain anymore and found myself negotiating in favor of his needs and desires. He hurt me to where I lost my self-esteem and self-worth. When, in fact, he was strange. He gossiped too much and was always around gay men at the garage. I was leery he may have been bisexual man he denied. He had serious commitment issues, which were toxic when dating. I had to draft a paper about the downward spiral of shame I experienced with him. Thankfully, I am an astute person with plenty of interests besides partners. Even still—during my darkest days when my heart was broken, in my profound, intimate worship, I felt abandoned.

No one pressured me to marry as much as I pressured myself about it when I was younger. I fantasized about walking down the aisle, wearing a beautiful wedding gown, and receiving precious gifts at a beautiful church. Once you realize a wedding is not a marriage, you can learn to appreciate it more. When you find the right partner who has learned the same lessons on the same timeline, you deeply respect and honor each other.

I once cared profoundly about what erodes a relationship. In releasing the reins, I allowed God to use His holy spirit to lead me. Whenever I do not follow, I reap the curse.

The pain just would not go away while I was in federal prison. There I was surrounded by both younger and older women serving thirty, forty, or fifty years. Some had life or double life sentences for standing behind a man for drugs. Meanwhile, I was in a relationship with Buno who had just divorced his spouse to start a family with me. We had two children together, though I refused his proposal for marriage three times. I was afraid our relationship would end—and it did. What you fear the most shall come upon you. He got involved with many women, but he married the woman who he liked best. She wanted a family after a previous divorce, even though she knew Buno was not the man she deserved. She did it because I was in prison. She is suffering now because the son they have together disrespects

Buno around mine and his daughter because it upsets him that there are other kids.

Buno's second wife so desperately wanted a relationship with him that she did not care who she hurt. She once told my daughter, to marry a decent man, she would need to dress better. Some guidance, huh!? The worst part was that my children kept this kind of stuff secret from me because they both were hurting and did not know or understand any of it. The wife refuse to support my daughter in her education who is now a nursing student. She got what she wanted in the end, and that was a lazy man who sold drugs and later worked part-time.

I promised Buno if he did not keep it real with me, I would take our kids away from him, move, and change the children's name to my married name. He was afraid of this, so he played house with his wife and tried for years to keep the kids from their siblings and me. It was painful and hurtful, even though I knew karma would come eventually. He and the spouse now both live with chronic illnesses. They struggle with obesity; they have cancer, diabetes, and other illnesses.

The worst thing he could have done was keep our babies away from me, and he knew it. He did the most forbidden thing. Out of fear, he and his wife tried to speak badly about me to our kids. They did not know what I could do to both. I had plans, but realized they were not worth the consequences.

When his spouse got sick with colon cancer and lupus, she was out of work for more than a year, and they did not want me to get even a whiff that she was in the hospital. Buno did the same thing with her as he did with me to get to her. She knows it and is comfortable with that reality. When you know God commands us to honor our spouses, but you stay in a marriage you know is not good, you are acting out of pure selfishness.

Then, there were haters who tried to compete with me. These relationships are just dead weight; they keep you sinking. There are people who do not tell you who they are before you ever involve yourself with them. Then again, I did not listen intently to the men I married. They both blamed their former girlfriends or wives for demeaning them, and I felt sorry for them at various times because I was self-concerned and bored. This was the only way to get my attention. If I had listened, I would have recognized the warning signs in the beginning. I was so busy being polite I disregarded their confessions. I failed to realize they both knew themselves better than I did. I did not think about what was in my best interest.

Buno told me what to expect, and yet I missed the signals. We had nothing in common; we were two broken and wounded souls pulled in different directions.

I had to learn Jesus's way to redemption. Our Lord's son had a team. He had a group of people with the same directional focus, even though they were dissimilar—a tax collector, a physician, a fisher man, and a prostitute. They all agreed on a destination. He did not choose all the same type of people. To unlock strength in their diversity, they had to step forward together. In many relationships and in churches, this unifying force through individual difference is destroyed when they try to make everyone act and feel the same.

Both men in my life were takers. Both took what they wanted from early in our partnership. Life has given me enough enemies to fight without also having to face the ghost lurking in the shadows of my mind. While running this race, I will give it my best. I hear voices that say I cannot do it. Like mold stuck to basement walls, regret breeds in dark places. The first thing I must leave behind is fear. It is the enemy of greatness—the opposite of faith. The longer it resided in me, the stronger it became. It is fertilized by the words you speak. It is the language you use to talk about yourself and leaves you shaking. The worst enemies to fight live within. I must rid my mind of fear, or it will defeat me each time. I had to learn when to say *hello* and *goodbye* to old issues, which otherwise threatened to stagnate me.

The choice will always be mine. I will choose what will cling to my soul and what I will dump. My soul must be effective for my life. I choose what I want to and what I must carry. Everything that has happened to me has spiritual significance given through God Himself. He intends to use even painful events for my good, even when Satan and others meant them for my doom.

Selfishness pervades our lives. Through trial and tribulation, I was yet tuned to a quiet, still voice of God. He finds a way to communicate; all I need to do is sit still with an expectant heart. I stripped away all thoughts of those who did me wrong, talked about me, or lied about me, and thus, I deny them to spin the composition of my life.

To follow God's plan, I walked past voices trying to distract me. I divorced myself from the tendency to live life selfishly. If I am going to win, I must realize all I have and hope for is at stake. After repeatedly hit in the face, I aim to win with conviction. All my moves must count. I had to strategically rise above catastrophes to make the best of my life. At a certain a point in my life, I said *enough is enough*.

I sabotaged my true greatness with hedonistic stupidity. I am no longer doing Department of Corrections time. However, the time I put into discovering what causes me to do what I do proves enormously difficult. Having the chance to learn about myself is worth all the years of blindness. It is worth being stuck in harmful family dynamics, dysfunctional patterns, unhealthy relationships, codependency, resentment, pain, self-sabotage, and neglect.

Nothing in life is to be feared, it is only to be understood.

—Marie Curie

In all my endeavors, I've learned karma comes to everyone no matter who they are. Only the strong survive. Life has taught me never to trust anyone with anything. I left my ex with a Range Rover, which was only three years old, and two beautiful homes he was afraid he wasn't ready for. I suggested he use a realtor to assist in renting one of the homes so it would help him out. Only unqualified, insecure men lose valuable property and need a woman to pay for all—or the bulk—of the expenses. I won notoriety in my case with the federal government—not everyone is afraid of. They play dirty for those in the drug game.

My Mother's Final Days

We cannot underestimate the vital importance of our life's decisions.

OUR MOTHER HAD A TERMINAL illness which no one knew about other than herself and my daughter Alexis. Alexis was thirteen when mother in secret told her not to tell anyone. Nine years later, her condition worsened.

Mother came home from work believing she had the flu. She lay in bed, asleep, she began to vomit. I could see over the course of resting; her stomach had swollen. She had to go to the ER while there a member of the hospital clergy ask if she have a pastor or a priest. We said yes and asked why.

He said she has stage four colon cancer, and he did not expect her to live. Mother did not care to hear this from him. She wanted to go home. Instead of facing mortality, she knew she needed rest from the job and the household. Still the hospital kept her one or two days. Of course, I was absorbed in knowing I would be losing my mother in this situation. The woman who gave birth to me was terminally ill, and the doctor had no hope.

I was in the process of relocating to a brownstone apartment in New York a friend of mine owned. He planned to rent it out to me so I could get away from family and drama. I lived about thirty-five minutes from Mother, and yes, I enjoyed my place when I was home. However, I decided to need to spend as much time as possible with Mother since Knuckie did not know how to care for anyone- never mind someone sick.

Mother knew she was in trouble, if Knuckie had to do it all alone, the arrangement would have worked out. I was always there six days on and one day off. I wanted to be with Mother seven days a week, yet I need some free time for myself to unwind. An ever-loving person, Mother was comfortable and enthusiastic about having my grandbaby, Dru, there with her. Dru was less than two years old at the time. He would give her a kiss and play with her everyday sipping out of her cup with a straw. He did it snakingly as he would walk away with her cup of ginger ale sip and look at her. She got a kick out of Dru, my grandson someone who brought mother joy and love every day until she passed.

Mother and I talked. I would tell her she would be fine, and I would be with her. She was able to walk, eat, go to the bathroom and to her doctor visits until her health began to decline all at once surprisingly. Mom was honest with me. I had to always come to her aid when her and Knuckie were at odds regarding her own money. Clearly, Knuckie stole and spent it. Still Mother never acted out of character. She remained perpetually a lady when overseeing her business. If she did not care to be around you, you would know. Together, we would listen to gospel, pray daily, watch TV, and have meals. I would wash her, comb her hair, and rub her body when she felt pain. A traditionalist, Mother held tight onto God's hand all the way. In her final stages, I asked her what she wanted to wear to heaven, and she already knew.

Mother did not believe in drugs, a fact which her family and friends took full advantage of. They stole all the Percocet, oxycodone, and morphine she had around the home. These people would stay the night and hang out all day while Mother enjoyed their company. She cared nothing for the meds- only prayer. After mom's passing there was yet many bottles of prescribed drugs she did not use. Most of the addicts around were stealing mom meds for their mental pain.

We decided to take Mother to get a second opinion. I had suggested this earlier, but Mother took no interest in the idea. She had placed all her trust in the One who can do all things. At Smilow Cancer Center at Yale, a new specialist began to treat Mother immediately. He asked her how badly she wished to live. She replied, "Badly."

Mother would sit up in her bed as I sat in a chair beside her. We shared what was going to happen and she shared what she expected from me. She wanted me to do well and never return to prison. She knew Knuckie's malicious behavior had escalated. Knuckie did not want me to inherit anything from Mother—nor did she want me to discover what she did with Mother's insurance policy. My sister had canceled the policies intended to benefit my younger brother and myself in the amount of $170,000. I did not know this until after mother was in the ground. Knuckie thought because she had lived with mother for thirty-five years, she was entitled to everything. Of course, she had also stolen the most from Mother. She even canceled or took ownership of all mother's other life insurance policies. Later, Knuckie found herself unable to pay and ended up losing them. I brought this to the magistrate's attention during our probate hearing, and again, she lied about it. Mother knew Knuckie always plotted. My sister constantly believed someone *else* was trying to get something from Mother.

Stories organize chaos, create content, and impose meaning. Like sensory experience, the details we see are meaningless until fathomed into narrative. My story is my destiny—it follows the path it needs to. So, everything depends on my power to shape my future. It is dysfunctional, and thus, I must identify it and rewrite it. My life is the most important story I will ever tell, and I am telling it right now.

For me, the book of Ruth connected the biblical dots to Jesus. Her narrative reminds me of my mother, who connected me to Jesus. I'm eternally grateful for this, which is a legacy in itself. My mother was a spiritual warrior.

Here is an important lesson we all should learn. It comes from Genesis 48:1-20.

The Bible tells of the health of Joseph's father Jacob, the family patri-arch, which was failing. Joseph took his two sons, Manasseh and Ephraim, to visit Jacob, who wanted to bless the boys as is custom. Traditionally, the first-born son receives twice as much inheritance or blessing. The patriarch places his right hand on the oldest son and left hand on the other. This was how Joseph presented them to Jacob. Manasseh was the first-born, so Joseph set him to his father's right and Ephraim to the left. When Jacob went to bless the two boys, he did something different. He stretched out his right hand and laid it on Ephraim's head, and he set his left hand on Manasseh's head.

Jacob switched hands, and so he broke the tradition.

No one expected this to happen, and though Joseph tried to stop him, Jacob insisted. His father's decision displeased Joseph entirely.

Yet, Jacob said, "I know, my son; I know. Manasseh will also become a great people, but his younger brother will become even greater. And his descendants will become a multitude of nations."

This lesson teaches us God looks at the heart and not the lineage. He always gives preference to those who are listening and following Him. In fact, the story of Jacob's sons echoes that of their father. Like them, Jacob received first blessing over his elder brother, Esau, who willingly traded his birthright.

The story of Cain and Abel also follows this pattern; although Cain was the first born, God saw Cain felt entitled and so gave preference to the offering of his brother Abel. God created all things to work together for the good of those who love Him.

Our mother knew I was able to care for myself, and she saw something more in me than she saw in Knuckie. I remember bishops, pastors, prophets, deacons of the church, and visitors would tell my mom I was gifted. I had a spirit of discernment, they said. I was not noisy, curious, or any of that—I just had a way of knowing what was going on inside of someone.

Seasons tell time. They hold one hostage like they do with ripening fruit and blooming trees. It is now my time. On so many occasions, the devil tried to block the release of the book you are reading, which I believe will help heal and encourage so many people. Know, dear reader, who God is and what He will do for you. Nothing is ever wasted. What may now stink in your life can someday elevate you. It may not smell good to you, but it will help you to grow in challenging times. When the world tries to stagnate you, God will move you forward. God doesn't waste anything He has used you for. It may not have been *good*, but God will make good out of it. Nothing is ever wasted—even the hurt and the pain.

You will defeat what was meant to defeat you. Challenges will come, but you can outlast them. People may think they are pushing you down when in fact they are pushing you up. One touch of God's favor will propel you.

Most people in church do not know God. They only know of what He can do as told by their leader. I need God to share His teachings. Even some of God's people, the parishioners, remain blind because they remain fixated on—and hide behind—designer clothes and other material goods.

When people talk about you, always correct them and tell the truth. Say *yes, it happened, but I did not do it with criminal intentions as the government said.* In my case, I created a successful business and made more money than others, which angered the government. They used it at their discretion to convict me. As for the people who committed crime, they allowed them to cooperate to win a conviction. I know I'm chosen when people lie about me; it demonstrates God's will to challenge me. Thus, he elevated my person. When people do not like you, they will tell a lie. One cannot be healed holding secrets.

In telling the truth, nothing can touch me. Sin is not attracted to anyone without a name. Sin wants to take your testimony. You cannot receive a miracle and keep secrets; once you are healed, the story can't hurt you. You cannot hurt me with what I have been delivered from. I claim my sin. It bears my name. You are whole when your perspective shifts and shame no longer accesses you.

In the degree that we remember and retell our stories and create new ones we become the authors, the authorities, of our own lives.

—Sam Keen

I get it. Knuckie does not like me, and that is her problem—not mine. At one time, I could not understand her animosity. We both came from the same mother and father. I now spiritually comprehend our relationship. We just had our own identities. Knuckie recently shared with me Mother always praised me to anger her.

I then replied and said, "You knew she was doing it to get you mad, and you got mad. She did not mean anything by it. You allowed this to bother you that bad."

Flustered, she could not defend herself. The devil beat her into a rage. I understand because the Holy Spirit gave me insight a few years ago. Reputation is what people place on you, and character is who I am. Why does God invest in me? He looks beyond my flaws.

We need to know why people are mad with us. My family, relatives, friends, ex-husband, ex-boyfriends, and others do not like me because I am more valuable than them. Each speck of dirt on me is worth more than their whole being. They thought my besmirched past diminished me, but because I survived, my value is higher. I am an overcomer. My coat alone inspired jealousy because daddy gave me a colorful life. Some of us are miracles among those who exist in ordinary lives.

Some of us are waiting on becoming our best selves. I continually strive for this from within a hole, without water, in 120 degrees. Still breathing, still living in dirt, someone found me, and I still have value. We all face this struggle. How are you making it?

The anointing will get your attention. You don't see it unless you ask God to show you.

—T.D. Jakes

Heroes take journeys, confront dragons, and discover the treasure of their true selves.

—Carol Pearson

For a long time, I lay in a hole—a dark prison. There, God gave me a dream, and in dreaming, I climbed. I saw what part I play in His plan. Early in life, I struggled, but God said there is still potential remaining.

We do not just hear God's voice; we hear the devil's voice, too. In God's word, we are taught to love our enemy, but not the devil.

Where you see dirt, I see fertilizer. I have more value in a hole than people who have never been in one. I have more value for having lived my life than people who have never made a mistake. Our real enemies do not know how praise set my path. I got away with so much. But, if not for the negotiator, Jesus, I would not have this chance to change. Jesus reminds me the dead cannot praise you. The miracle is the power to admit I did it! What should have been my funeral is now my future.

I will not give up on God. I will receive the grace He has for me. I believe God rules over my life. I know God takes care of my business in His time. I am highly favored.

We cosmetically cover to spiritually cover our insecurities. We dress and adorn ourselves with Gucci, Fendi, Versace, and Louis Vuitton. We conceal our pain with Christian Louboutin, Giuseppe, Zanotti, or Stuart Weizmann heals, nouveau lashes, long hair, and MAC makeup.

Some think driving a foreign car elevates one's status, even though their girlfriend has Section 8 housing, and there is no garage to park the foreign car in. Go to school, work, learn as much as you can and stay faithful to God in prayer. He will see you through.

The events in my life work harmoniously with God's plan. He blended them together for my good. God could have kept Joseph, Paul, and me out of jail. But in challenging us, He brings good out of the worst evil, and each of us drew closer to God for it. From my sins to my mistakes, my disappointments, my trauma, my pain, my debt, the deaths of loved ones, my divorce, disasters, and illnesses—all of it serves God.

Paul said, "We know that these troubles produce patience, and patience produces character."

For the present, I will continue to honor and praise God. My circumstances won't last forever. When I outlive these trials, I'll thank Him. Prayer is significant!

Prayer releases the favor of God for us, in us, and through us. I had to realize prayer won't improve my relationship with my children unless I work at it.

I am a person I kept locked away for many years. I had to discover a way to deal with my harmful feelings without a clue. How do I free her. My path now in perspective. My past serves to teach, rather than define me. Even when I recognize the prejudice I faced, I can find happiness because I know I'm not alone. We are all wounded, all healing, and all in the process of growing. When we look beyond prejudgment, we see the potential for growth in others. As a convicted felon, I see how our prejudice challenges us as a society to respond to ex-offenders in a more human and intelligent way.

As for me, from my best times to my worst times, I've stood tall and praised the all-knowing God. Even during my most difficult periods, God has blessed me to do the impossible. Most of what I share comes from the values, morals, and principles I learned from my parents and grandparents, and some comes from certainty that this compelling story is embedded deep in my psyche. For the first time, I embrace the full concept of empowerment by learning about myself, from whom I ran my entire life.

Today, I have grandchildren I love dearly. I live for them and hope like hell I always remember that in everything I do, so I never, ever leave them again. To God be the glory, hallelujah! My grandchildren look up to me, love me, and cherish me. It's a wonderful feeling. I'm overjoyed to see them receive the nurturing I didn't get. In this way, I know my actions were meaningful. With my genes, they're truly, amazingly ingenious children. And we don't have any of Trump's stolen money to live off! I hope my demanding work and sweat will allow them to flourish. I have an appointment with destiny! Like David, God lifted me from obscurity to notoriety.

The real struggle for me is to shrug off my old man's hustling lifestyle. Unfortunately, my values are all corrupt because of my habitual mentality, where deceitfulness and lust made their home. Change takes a while because of how long my habits lasted.

True power, as I've come to learn, increases the more you embody truth. I will embrace my unique path of growth, and I will use my intellect and emotions to guide me in the conscious pursuit of truth, love, and power. The greatest gift you give the world is to share who you really are and accept the highs and lows, which are equally valuable. I recognize my deepest sorrows reveal my greatest joy. I will share my stories with others and know I am not alone. I cancel, abolish, and demolish every territory of the enemy and every plot against me.

Devil, if you come through the waters, I command liquid to freeze you.

Devil, if you come through the trees, I command the vines to bar you.

God will create a situation I would have never got in myself. *Vengeance is mine*; He will say. For a while, it will look as if nothing is happening, but this is the way God works. Just because judgment isn't executed speedily, it doesn't mean justice won't come. God makes changes on a generational scale, which will help my children, grandchildren, and great-grandchildren. When everything I misrepresented shifts in my favor, I will realize it's my time, my hour, to receive my moment. My ugliness have been addressed.

This is my year. I am going to turn it around. *This is my year!* Devil, you are a liar. You tried to kill me. You tried to destroy me. You tried to drive me crazy, and you tried to have me eat dirt. I am here to tell you I am back.

My way of thinking reflects where I came from. I cannot fathom how I can be saved and struggle with the economic disparities and challenges of the neighborhood where I grew up. Through God, I no longer expect the same things out of life. As God continues to transform my mind, a river of change flows bearing my name. Nothing is beyond our reach! Praise God! I must give God the glory for my resurrection—for giving me my joy back.

God shined a light on me. As it heated, it reminded me how media personnel and a writer followed my arrest record. The writer wrote what he wanted about me simply for the publication of his stories. Above whom he hurt, he valued what he said in his own terms. A woman is not her crime. We all have someone in our bloodline with serious issues they keep quiet out of embarrassment, but I'm not ashamed to admit the things which most embarrass me. I'm built from more than the worst parts of my life!

God delivered me from my father's bondage. The devil placed me in sin, yet Jesus came back to get me. He redeemed my empty life. He was able to set me free from my parents.

Pain allows you to nurture your worth, and you keep your value alive. I had to learn to release any and all pain like it never existed. To this end, I learned haters cannot stop destiny. All negative gossip about me serves God's divine purpose. The Bible tells us one suffers before God picks us up.

People tend to believe what they hear from the media. The narrative they report is always one step removed from the reality of the situation. In retelling a story, there is often nuance lost or more meaning implied than is the case. As individuals and as consumers of media, we need to decide what to believe. When I reflect on these ideas, of what was going on in with our democracy under the forty-fifth president's administration. That POTUS and his cabinet committed crimes with impunity. It was a disgrace. It was a disgrace former AG Bill Barr, allegedly blocked investigations for a thief. They all knew their actions to be wickedness with the intent to do wrong. We saw judges and justices whom ill will play a critical role because the POTUS told them to do so. The sequence of events during this presidency made folks think the world was imminently approaching what is foretold in the Book of Revelation. I was continually and utterly disappointed with this president.

I paid more than my dues when the prosecutors in state and federal courts gave me entirely too much time. Excessive punishment like this causes people to dislike, even hate, those who work in the system. Their motivation is, transparently, to protect their own. This world is cruel and unjust toward the Black race. Yet, in my trials and case hearings, I sometimes thought I deserved my treatment because of all the trouble I'd gotten myself in for those early years. Still, I evaded prison for a long time, and the longer I did, the uglier my situation became. The government tenaciously pursued my imprisonment, and that is something I will never forget. The people in power always made my actions appear maximally malicious. Over time, the words of others transform the picture we have of ourselves. Adding to the harm, the government uses a target's family or friends to pad thin cases. What they do is use Black people to accomplish their goals. I, and many people I know, witnessed the judicial system in action, and it blatantly demonstrated to us how corrupt President Trump and his administration really was, such as during the first senate trial. I saw it for myself.

We must do what is right. We must teach our children the tools to navigate the system and how it works. The bleak reality is—those who run this country will never do the right thing.

Tradition begins in one visionary, who then passes it down. If nurtured, traditions can become an endowment, which permeate the soul of many generations. Prison changed me in ways I did not anticipate, and I now hope my new way of engagement others will follow.

I'm working diligently toward positive change in the face of daunting odds. Meanwhile, I'm also extremely concerned about the diminished value of those headed to prison. Those who were convicted, sent to prison, and those who were convicted but not sent to prison are those who will continue to do what they do because of who they believe they truly are—trapped in their situations and in themselves.

Despite all these challenges, I remain optimistic about the future, particularly about future elections. No matter what negativity others cast, I will support candidates who pledge to positive change. I trust some candidates are decent human beings. We all fall short and repent for our sins accepted by Christ.

Acknowledgments

You will find peace not trying to escape your problems, but by confronting them courageously. You will find peace not in denial, but in victory.

—J. Donald Walters

I APPRECIATE THE MANY GREAT people who have helped me make this book possible. The are only a few who stood by me during my tribulations. To my late mother Clarice Halloway Bell-Wilson you are forever living with me, and I miss you so much. My husband Henry L. Price for giving me the courage and the stance to continue. My son Daryl has weathered through storms with me and has always been there for me and our family. My son Andrew, who fought his personal battles with me gave it his best. My daughter Alexis and son Joshua were always present and understood me in a way I wish everyone could. I will always remember my daughter Willean who is willing to give me a chance. And my son Donald who is yet growing who will find his way to me on God's time. To late Elder Lee Roy Mc Coy, a true man of God- thank you for your insight encouragement, and many prayers. Late Pastor Jean Knapp taught me to trust God no matter what.

I thank my children who I am indebted too, my Attorney F. Mac Buckley who's stupendous who's knowledge pushed me, my mentor and Attorney Jim Higgins, who saw my potential when I thought it waned. The Laborer's International Union of North America (LIUNA) helped me enormously. I especially honor the board, all the instructors and secretary who gave me their undivided diligence in the construction trade, and the VP of

LIUNA, Armand Sabitoni, an amazing man who is always looking out for others. Finally Wally Lamb—I could not forget all you did to make it possible for me to be in your writing group and the members of your team.

I now gratefully view myself differently, with all the skills and unique perspective I possess. I can face challenges with my best effort. I successfully operated a company that I never thought possible after learning the construction trade. I did not know I made it happen. Never did I become complacent in this industry. It was through challenging work I enjoyed my paychecks. It was so uncomfortable wearing a half facemask respirator while working in the Covvid-19 pandemic, which has spread globally. Allegedly, it was said it claimed hundred of thousands of lives. No vaccine is expected to be available until at least a year following the virus spread. This virus has caused the biggest unemployment and business loss in a decade, the economic impact of which some say is worse during the Great Depression.

I especially would like to thank the devil, his demons, cohorts and emps for keeping me on my knees, praying, and lifting my hands to God with praise!

If you treat a woman as she is, she will stay as she is, but if you treat her as she ought to be and could be, she will become as she ought to be , and could be ad more. If I had remained full of doubt and depress, there would not have been people to benefit from my stories. It is only with my shared experiences I am able to help others, just being born makes me worthy enough to be here. I am responsible for my life.

It is important to know why I was programmed to feel the way I did. I have now done the work of changing the program. Early on, I may have judged myself unworthy. This is one of the most important challenges of my life- to heal the wounds of my past so I do not continue to bleed. I have dragged the weight of my trauma into my future, which made it impossible for me to move forward. My life is a multi-part series of all my experiences, where each event I created by my thoughts, actions and intentions. Each teaches me what I need to know. The god news is, I am not perfect. When you don't know who you are, chances are you don't know what you want.

And when someone does not know what they want, there isn't any chance they'll get it. I created my stories according to truth. The best way to learn is by falling. I was born a writer.

A writer prepares herself as an actor with vulnerability. She shows everything about herself to her readers through the filter of one's character, priorities, needs, and desires. When I am stuck, I must free myself without help. Complaining may offer relief and acceptance does, too. There is no perfect life. Eventually, I'll settle into personal satisfaction and no reason to complain will remain.

I am who I am. I am not my crime. I accept myself as I am. I have created my stories according to the truth, not to hurt anyone, but to tell my story.

The best way to learn anything is by falling. God will guide us through our hardship. As I end my stories, there must be something better. The devil is busy. I received a call recently and was told Knuckie *did it again*. The devil is a liar! I am self-surrendering to authorities today for bail. Her boyfriend has not been home a week, and already, boredom has seized control. I genuinely feel that Knuckie misses me. In December of 2019, a detective called me to ask if I could meet with her because the department was doing an investigation on tools. She said Knuckie called constantly to try to have me arrested.

I said, "All right. I'm working now, so it'll have to be after." At the time, I was working far from my usual jobs. The day of our meeting, I was running late, and I called her to say I could not make it. Besides, I didn't really care about Knuckie and her nonsense. Her boyfriend was in prison again. I left a message on her voicemail to say we could meet another day. I arrived home to tell my children, who cared about Knuckie no more than I. Two of my children said they would not go if they were me. What they would do is fabricate something since she constantly went out of her way concerning me. It made sense my life busy with my grandkids. I now taking advise from my daughter who later told me she committed this crime feeling bad in my face using the checks of a bum with no money on a closed account wow! Not anything I would do not my mo. I will not be able to reschedule, nor will I be coming. I have been told to stay off Twitter by love ones.

My conscience tells me former AG Bill Barr may have something to do with this arrest, since I'm always on social media blasting him, Trump, Mitch McConnell, and the rest of the crooks. This world is cruel, and so are the people in it. Those on the top are dangerous. As Jadakiss says in his song "Pearly Gates"— "The journey is for the chosen. Throughout it all, all I can do is remain golden."

Finally, be strong in the Lord and His mighty power. Put on the full armor of God, so that you can take your stand against the devil's schemes. For our struggle is not against flesh and blood, but against the rulers, against the authorities, against the powers of this dark world and against the spiritual forces of evil in the heavenly realms. Therefore, put on the full armor of God, so that when the day of evil comes, you may be able to stand your ground, and after you have done everything, to stand. Stand firm then, with the belt of truth buckled around your waist, with the breastplate of righteousness in place, and with your feet fitted with the readiness that comes from the gospel of peace. In addition to all this, take up the shield of faith, with which you can extinguish all the flaming arrows of the evil one. Take the helmet of salvation and the sword of the Spirit, which is the word of God.

And pray in the Spirit on all occasions with all kinds of prayers and requests. With this in mind, be alert and always keep on praying for all the Lord's people.

—Ephesians 6:10-18, NIV

I have experienced it all, but I never expected to see what is transpired in this cruel world for our democracy. Still, I am blessed to witness our forty-sixth president lead our country away from what would have been total corruption. Do I accept corruption of any kind, or do I use my voice? We are powerful beyond what we can imagine. Wars and rumors of war called forth memories of those my grand mom told us about as kids. We sat around her as she peeled and cut potatoes and fresh green beans while giving us the word of God. It was all she knew.

As I look forward, I see fresh hope. Protestors for Black Lives Matter against police brutality and against racism fill me with optimism. As for myself, I have found peace in recognizing I can only control my own actions. I cannot control former partners any more than I can my sister. Finally, I hope these stories provide my children and grandchildren with the insight into who I am. And what they did not get because of my time in prison. May they serve others in their personal, and spiritual, journeys.

We Him And I Communicate The Things We Are Most Embarrassed To Admit

"My Wife Is A Thief"